THE
HAPPINESS
INDEX

THE HAPPINESS INDEX

Why Today's Employee Emotions Equal Tomorrow's Business Success

MATT PHELAN

WILEY

For general information on our other products and services or for technical support, please contact our Customer Care Department within the United States at (800) 762-2974, outside the United States at (317) 572-3993 or fax (317) 572-4002.

Wiley also publishes its books in a variety of electronic formats. Some content that appears in print may not be available in electronic formats. For more information about Wiley products, visit our web site at www.wiley.com.

Library of Congress Cataloging-in-Publication Data is Available:

ISBN 9781394166602 (Cloth)
ISBN 9781394166619 (ePub)
ISBN 9781394166626 (ePDF)

Cover Design: Joe Wedgwood
Cover Image: © fenskey/Adobe Stock

SKY10052228_072823

I would like to dedicate this book to my partner, Liz, and our amazing children, Izzy and Fred. Our children challenge us every day in so many beautiful ways.

The tears, the laughter. The ups, the downs.

All of it.

I hope that years from now, when Izzy and Fred are adults, they will read the words on this page and think to themselves:

"Maybe he wasn't actually that embarrassing after all?!"

Contents

Acknowledgments

EMPLOYEES

I would like to acknowledge every single person I have ever employed.

I was 25 when we first started employing people. I had got by on a £2,000 loan from the bank and a few side jobs at the start and it was about 6 months into the business that our customer fees allowed us to start employing people. I was dreadfully unprepared to be a manager.

It has been a long, hard 15-year journey with plenty of mistakes made along the way, but we strive to learn from all of these relationships and to improve.

Where I was incredibly fortunate was having the most amazing mum, who taught me what leadership is about. As an immigrant working mum with five young children, my mum somehow always made time for people. Time to listen, not to judge or to offer random bits of advice. Just to listen.

Some people laugh when I say this, but I put employing someone right up there on par with marriage in terms of responsibility. When you recruit someone, you enter into an arrangement where the decisions you make can positively or negatively shape the future of that individual. Everything you do has an impact on them, from their financial prospects to their mental health.

For this relationship to work, it needs to be a partnership and work as a two-way street. If both partners work hard on that relationship, what you can achieve together is limitless.

My learning from these relationships is that you get out what you put in. Listen to people and they will listen to you. Be loyal to people and they will be loyal to you. Give people the tools to succeed and they will succeed.

However the flip is also true. Don't listen to your employees and they won't listen to you. Treat your employees like a number on a spreadsheet and they will treat employment as a purely transactional arrangement.

The joy and happiness that can be gained from a group of people coming together to work on something big, bold, and scary is one of the most incredibly rewarding endeavors available to us.

Jackie Dyal, one of my colleagues at the Happiness Index introduced a really simple process to The Happiness Index called a retro. It is a simple daily routine asking two questions:

What went well? What could have we improved on?

As founders we don't get things right all the time and we are far from perfect. I often reflect in these retros on moments and situations as an employer that I wish had gone better from the last 15 years. I try to learn from all my experiences of being an employer and improve step by step.

Thank you to everyone who has been on the journey over the last 15 years through all the lows and the highs.

EXPERT CONTRIBUTORS

I am a huge believer in the idea that for humanity to thrive, we need to combine data, research, and storytelling. In this book I invited 25 experts to bring together some of this data and research into practical advice you can use today.

Thank you to this collective of 25 amazing storytellers from across the world. I am lucky to know you and thankful that our careers have crossed whilst researching this book: Sope Agbelusi, Natasha Wallace, Phil Burgess, Matthew Knight, Hannah Litt, Jenn Lim, Cathy Courtenay, Laura Page, Arlette Bentzen, Simon Berry, Margot Slattery, Karen Robinson, Rob Turner, John Fitzgerald, Minter Dial, Kevin Withane, Fiona McDonnell, Dan Sodergren, Steven Bianchi, Andrew MacAskill, Ben RainforthGott, Njabulo Mashigo, Clive Hyland, and Tony Latter.

CITED RESEARCH

There are now over 223,560 research papers on employee engagement and happiness. It was incredibly difficult to whittle this down to 40 or so papers that would help readers on their learning journey.

Thank you to everyone doing research in this area, and a shoutout to all the experts specifically mentioned in this book: When writing a book, there are always a few amazing people who deserve a special mention.

Gemma Shambler, our head of people, for practicing what we preach and putting all of what we discussed in this book into action. We don't always get things right but we are always committed to learning and improving.

Clive Hyland, our head of neuroscience, for helping us bridge the scientific community and the work community. Clive's role in helping us use the latest science and making it accessible to all of us is something we are incredibly fortunate and thankful for.

Tony Latter, my co-founder, was an incredibly great person to speak to when I was suffering from the dreaded writer's block. Tony helped me write, rewrite, and reshape key sections of this book.

Amanda Marksmeier, for writing up all the expert podcasts and pulling all the external research together. If you enjoy any of the experts in this book, you can find their full interview on the Happiness and Humans podcast.

Patrick Phelan (My actual brother) who joined us before we had money to employ people. Pat is known by most of our customers as the calm core of the business. Pat has been keeping a weekly customer diary that he writes to the company every Friday on insight that he has learnt from working with our customers.

He calls his Friday email "Pat's nuggets" and these nuggets were a goldmine (pun intended) when writing the customer insights in the 8 core chapters of this book.

Joe Wedgwood, our brand and design manager, for the designs in this book and the cover, all of which is Joe's amazing creative work.

A final thank-you to our community of readers of my previous book for encouraging me to write a second book, and for all the feedback on everything from cover design to the name of this book.

Foreword

It's been seven years since I joined The Happiness Index, which at the time was just a start-up. I was the first employee—or 001, the tongue-in-cheek name I gave myself! Since then the company has grown to help organizations measure their culture in over a hundred countries.

It may sound cliché, but it really has been a roller coaster of a journey! It's quite unusual for a millennial to remain with a company for as long as I have, but the reason for working here is purpose-driven. It has been a passion of mine to help people. When I was younger this was done via charity events or helping communities, but I never felt that was enough.

It hadn't occurred to me that I could do this on a larger scale, until an opportunity to work at The Happiness Index arose, helping organizations to look after their employees.

I'd experienced working for other organizations that weren't people focused and—in each role—within six months I had my eye on the door. Those experiences helped me to understand some of the reasons why it's crucial to look after your people and give them a voice. This was a significant driver for me to enable this within other organizations.

I don't want other employees to be deeply unhappy at work like I was. I want them to thrive and bring the best version of themselves to work because it's only through doing this that they'll flourish.

When I tell people I work at The Happiness Index, people assume I'm always happy, but as you'll see from the data in this book, it's impossible to be happy 100% of the time.

There will always be peaks and troughs, and it's in those troughs that you learn and grow. That collective intelligence is what informs the direction our customers strive toward, and the changes that need to be made to create a happy, engaged, and successful organization.

During my time here, I've worked with a diverse range of organizations of varying sizes and industries. We have found that it's common for companies to have some of the same issues, irrespective of size or industry. But what is most important is ensuring that well-informed actions are taken to improve employee experience.

This is something we do internally at The Happiness Index, as well as with our customers—and there is nothing better than seeing employee engagement and happiness increase!

I have seen first-hand that being happy at work not only helps improve team performance, but on a personal level can radically transform your entire life in so many positive ways.

I'm excited about the future and to be able to share what we've learned from our neuroscience-designed platform in this book. Not only will it help you improve the happiness and engagement of your employees, but it will also increase your organization's chance of success.

This book will explore the different themes that make up our vision, "Freedom to be Human," something that I am passionate about and that drives me daily.

I feel very lucky to work for a company actively practicing this ethos, because it allows my colleagues and me to bring our true selves to work every day. This empowers me to be authentic in each aspect of my role, which I believe comes across when working with colleagues and clients. It creates a culture of openness and encourages a diversity of opinions within the business.

Personally, this allows me to work in a way that works for me. Having flexibility in the way I work is crucial to my happiness and well-being. I'm able to speak up and drive change where I see fit, and the flat structure allows for collaboration across the business.

I hope you enjoy this book, written by Matt Phelan, one of the co-founders of The Happiness Index. He's a great manager and an inspiring leader!

I will now hand over to Matt to share what we have learned along the way.

—Roma Varma, Employee 001 at The Happiness Index

CHAPTER 1

Introduction

Imagine for a moment we stopped seeing our emotions as weakness or simply something we need to control. What if every emotion you are currently feeling as you read these words on this page is intelligence to help you navigate life?

What would happen if we stopped ignoring this internal intelligence system that has evolved over thousands of years to help us grow?

Hello, and welcome to my new book! This book will explain how today's emotions are tomorrow's performance.

Before I introduce myself, I thought it would be useful to share a simple four-step guide for your journey through the book.

Guide 1: The Starting Point
We all need to face some key truths before we're able to make real change:

- Every organization in the world has unhappy employees.
- Every single human being has happiness levels that fluctuate.
- No company will ever have happy employees all the time.
- It is not healthy or realistic for human beings to be happy all the time.

Guide 2: Toxic Positivity and Perfection
This book is not about toxic positivity, perfection, or shoving happiness memes or tropes down your throat until you believe them. You can't simply "think" yourself into happiness. A positive outlook in life is a handy tool—research proves how

handy it is. However, this is not a positive psychology book. There are already loads of them (of varying quality).

The Happiness Index is not called *The "High" Happiness Index* for a reason. It is called an index because information from the highs and lows is equally important.

I have never met a perfect company or a leader who makes 100% spot-on decisions all the time. There is no one-size-fits-all strategy for a thriving culture, but there is data and insight that can help guide us all.

Our organization—The Happiness Index—and our customers struggle with all the factors we discuss in this book just as much as everyone else. However, having the data and insight I am about to share as a guiding light helps us improve our decision-making.

As a reader myself, when I pick up a book, I hope I'll learn the one perfect answer that I can take away and apply to my organization. Unfortunately, the world doesn't work like that. Like you, we at The Happiness Index don't get it right all the time, but we are able to make more informed decisions due to our data.

The starting point is that we must embrace all our feelings and thoughts to thrive.

Guide 3: Use-By Date
This book is about understanding the latest science, data, and research that drives employee engagement and happiness in the workplace so organizations can create the conditions for their employees to thrive and therefore their organizations to succeed.

The Happiness Index has measured the happiness levels of over two million human beings. However, the minute we collected that data it was out of date. That doesn't mean we can't learn from that data, but no data set that complex is ever going to be simple.

People love data because it can be used as fact. I don't see data as fact. I simply see it as what happened in one moment in time. Please use the data and research in this book to "make better decisions" not to "make decisions." Data is there to inform and help guide us.

Guide 4: Creating a Thriving Culture Takes Hard Work

There is no simple shortcut to a thriving culture. Employee happiness is a two-way street—it requires employees and organizations to contribute for it to work.

This book is for organizations that want to stop just saying their "people are their greatest asset" and start proving it. This book aims to give you a starting point and help guide you when creating a thriving workplace culture.

With those four guiding points established, let's all take a deep breath and relax into the book.

MY NAME IS MATT

Although this is my second book (my other book is *Freedom to Be Happy: The Business Case for Happiness*), I don't really see myself as an author. Although the words you are reading right now are written by me to you, the reader, I primarily see my role as your guide to help navigate what we have learned.

This book showcases amazing scientists, HR professionals, CEOs, professors, data scientists, practitioners, and storytellers, who all deserve huge credit for adding their unique perspectives to this story.

For some, data and research can be a dry subject. But thanks to the flair, passion, and research of the experts in this book, I'm able to bring the subject of employee engagement and happiness alive in a way that feels real and usable.

Today I am simply your tour guide who has pulled this book together for you while doing my two other jobs, the best and second-best jobs in the world:

- I am a dad.
- I work in happiness.

I do the morning school run five days a week, so by the time I start my normal workday I can be pretty flustered (well, full-on knackered, if I'm being completely honest). It's the best and worst part of my day. Doing the school run is one of my non-negotiables in my career and is a big part of my happiness.

It might sound odd that one of the most important things that drives my happiness also makes me feel stressed. The ancient Greeks would have understood my duality of emotions. They broke happiness down into what they called eudaimonia and hedonism.

EUDAIMONIA AND HEDONISM

Eudaimonia is that underlying, consistent feeling in life that you are happy or unhappy (the part of the school run that makes me happy). *Hedonism* or joy is the part of life that fluctuates daily with the ebbs and flows of life (in my life the part of the school run that can be stressful). These different feelings are a very normal part of being a living and breathing human being.

So although the school run does not necessarily bring me joy, it does bring me what I would describe as underlying life happiness.

Joy is supposed to go up and down like a healthy heartbeat. We are not programmed to live life in a constant state of joy or in a constant state of sadness. Your child forgetting their lunchbox and then having a tantrum in the middle of the street is not necessarily going to bring you joy.

Interestingly, many academics who have been guests on my podcast, "Happiness and Humans," prefer the term *subjective well-being* to *happiness*. It has been politely explained to me that happiness and subjective well-being are used interchangeably in research when referring to happiness. I am also told that subjective well-being is preferred because it helps their research be taken more seriously by governments and the people who award funding to universities (keep that one a secret between us).

In my last book, *Freedom to Be Happy: The Business Case for Happiness,* I comprehensively explored the concept that happiness is a pretty serious business metric, so we are not going to make a business case for happiness again in this book. As I write this, there are approximately 5,561 research papers on employee happiness and 218,000 on employee engagement, so around 223,561 incredibly rich sources of information.

If you still have doubts about happiness being a real metric, please check out *Freedom to Be Happy,* and read about how happier employees are more productive, more creative, sell more, and create better financial outcomes for their organizations.

I'm going to assume you are not applying for an academic research grant, so for the remainder of our journey, I will now simply refer to that normal up-and-down daily feeling we all experience every single day as *joy* and that underlying feeling of our happiness as *happiness*.

When I am not with family and friends, you can find me at The Happiness Index as co-CEO of the organization I co-founded in 2014. Its goal is to measure employee engagement, employee happiness, and organizational culture.

I love my job—I actually do.

Introducing This Book

So why a second book? Never say *never*.

After saying I would "probably *never* write another book again" at the book launch of *Freedom to Be Happy,* I have written another book.

Why?

I wrote my first book in the middle of a pandemic. Now, as we move into a new era, the world has changed forever. Many leaders moved into their senior roles at a pre-pandemic point in history. They have an experience bias based on a pre-pandemic world, a past and a reality that—unless Marty McFly and Doc Brown are going to knock on your door—is not coming back.

Right now, we have a unique opportunity to change the world, but there is simply not enough information to help organizations make informed decisions. Let me correct myself—there is enough research; it is all just hidden in plain sight beneath thousands of Google searches.

When under pressure, human beings go back to what they know best. The past can be a cozy, safe space that makes us feel comfortable. Nostalgia is an incredibly powerful force that can have both positive and negative outcomes on all our lives. Comfort is a nice feeling, but if we stay in our comfort zones for too long, we can lose opportunities to grow.

I wrote this book to share happiness and engagement information that can help bring employees and employers together and shape a positive future of work where we can all grow together.

So what are you about to read about?

If the number of social media followers is a proxy for influence, I will start by mentioning happiness quotes from three of the most followed people in the world on Instagram. Let's take a look at what Oprah Winfrey, Cristiano Ronaldo, and Kylie Jenner say about happiness:

> *Making other people happy is what brings me happiness. I have a blessed life, and I have always shared my life's gifts with others. I will continue to use my voice and my life as a catalyst for encouraging people to help make a difference in the lives of others.*
>
> **—Oprah Winfrey**

> *It's to have my family and my friends and to try to be the most happy person in the world.*
>
> **—Cristiano Ronaldo**

> *Happiness is a choice, not a result. Nothing will make you happy until you choose to be happy. No person will make you happy unless you decide to be happy.*
>
> **—Kylie Jenner**

Great quotes, but they are really a summary of three individuals' lived experiences that are very different from the billions of other people on this Earth.

HAPPINESS IS IN FASHION

Celebrities aren't the only ones who have been discussing happiness recently.

The world of work has suddenly started embracing employee happiness like a shiny, cool new thing to talk about to drive performance. If it was the 1980s, the switchboard would be going off just like at the *Ghostbusters* HQ. *"Ghostbusters hotline, how can we help you?"*

Over the last few years, it has become fashionable to talk about employee happiness. But at the same time, for some reason people have started talking less about employee engagement. My company had a small part to play in that but I don't think we were the only reason.

To ignore employee engagement is as dangerous as ignoring employee happiness has been for the last 30 years.

This increased interest in happiness is more likely coming from the symptoms of ignoring our human needs, the consequences of which are record levels of workplace bullying,[1] career burnout,[2] employee discrimination,[3] and suicide.[4]

YouGov states that 29% of UK workers report being bullied last year

CIPHR states that 36% of employees feel they've been subject to discrimination

Indeed states that 52% of employees have experienced burnout

The Samaritans put the UK Suicide rate at 1 in 10,000

Why is this happening? Simply rebranding employee engagement as employee happiness is not the answer. Employee engagement and happiness are now two very different areas. Just as different species evolved on Darwin's Galápagos Islands, employee engagement and employee happiness have evolved separately over time and focus on very different areas.

Clive Hyland, the head of neuroscience at The Happiness Index, describes employee engagement as what our brain needs and employee happiness as what our heart needs to thrive at work.

Both are equally important.

Going back to the academic definition of happiness or subjective well-being, the London School of Economics describes it as "How people think and feel about their lives and their everyday experiences." I really like this definition.

We describe engagement as what our brains think about our work and happiness as what our heart feels about work. But what does that actually mean, and what insight can we learn from the latest data?

To succeed in work and in life, we need to reconnect our brain with our heart. The data in this book can help you do that.

Many professionals use a social media tool called LinkedIn; a quick skim will reveal business professionals either sharing happiness quotes that inspire them or sharing advice on how to build a strong work culture. Don't get me wrong, these quotes are interesting, but we must remember that a quote is often based on one individual's lived experience. By all means be inspired, but don't fall into a trap of thinking that the quote is representative or should be followed like a map in your organization. Some of these quotes are repeated so much that they become taken as fact despite having no more data behind them than one influential person's point of view.

In this book, we move from individual perspectives on happiness to universal human truths so you can learn about what makes people tick.

DATA IS SIMPLY THE PLURAL OF ANECDOTE

Data is one tiny anecdote from one moment in time. When you combine all of these anecdotes into one dataset, you can start to learn about human behavior.

This book shares with you the data and insight gathered from over 2 million employees in over 100 countries. I also use research from 223,561 happiness and engagement external research studies, 24 in-depth expert interviews, and a deeper qualitative sample of 22,000 employees.

The amount of data and research can be quite overwhelming, so in each of the core eight chapters, I break this down and point you toward the key information to start your learning journey:

- Full descriptions of each happiness and engagement driver
- Live examples from organizations on the front line
- Key data shared from The Happiness Index dataset
- Featured external research
- Expert opinions from specialists on each of the 24 sub-drivers (see the image that follows)

I also provide you with a further research reading list in the bibliography for those eager to delve deeper. Note that the customers are all anonymous because their culture work is ongoing and all of them are working hard every day to create the conditions for their employees to thrive.

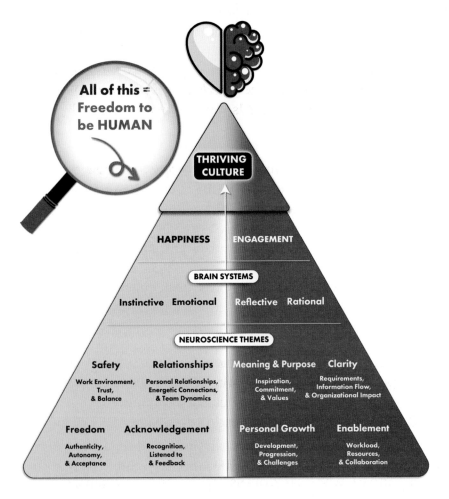

I must also point out that this data is collected from some of the most forward-thinking companies in the world. Companies that don't care about employee happiness simply don't work with the pink-and-yellow company called The Happiness Index.

The reason I share this is that you are about to start delving into data that is at an incredibly high benchmark. If we had data from all the organizations in the world, I think the picture would be much bleaker.

As stated, our customers still have plenty of unhappy employees; the only difference is they are prepared to do something about it.

We are now going to take a dive deep into the human condition and something we call the *freedom to be human*. What does this phrase actually mean? Is it a marketing slogan, like Nike's "Just do it"?

Freedom to be human means to be happy and engaged at work. Traditionally, companies want engaged employees and employees want to be happy. This book explores how neither side needs to compromise. It shows you how happy and engaged employees are a win-win for employees and organizations across the globe.

Thank you for picking up this book. I hope you enjoy it.

Notes

1. According to Trades Union Congress, nearly a third of people are bullied at work, https://www.tuc.org.uk/news/nearly-third-people-are-bullied-work-says-tuc
2. https://uk.indeed.com/lead/preventing-employee-burnout-report
3. https://www.ciphr.com/workplace-discrimination-statistics/
4. https://www.samaritans.org/about-samaritans/research-policy/suicide-facts-and-figures/latest-suicide-data/

A lot has changed since my co-founders and I started The Happiness Index in 2014. People starting a business are often told that it's really important to speak to their target market first. But it's not always that simple when trying to create a new market or category like happiness at work.

As Henry Ford famously said, "If I asked people what they wanted, they would have asked for faster horses."

When we started a happiness business, we were not just trying to innovate an existing market; we were trying to build a new market and encourage organizations to take emotions at work seriously. Happiness was still regularly described as the "soft side of business" or as a "fluffy metric." That's how the Employee Engagement and Happiness Platform came about.

Our Employee Engagement and Happiness Platform measures the entire employee experience, from onboarding to the day an employee leaves the organization. Years on, with customers using this platform in over 100 countries, we recount these stories with fond memories. At the time, we doubted if we could convince people that happiness had a place in the boardroom.

The start of our journey wasn't an easy one. . . .

Birthday Beginnings
In May 2014, we started The Happiness Index on my birthday (entrepreneurs are weird, I know) while sitting around a table with my daughter Izzy on my lap.

We were excited and convinced we had started a business that could make a positive impact on the world. To get some advice, we came up with a list of CEOs who might potentially use our platform and asked them for feedback.

THE FIRST CALL

I made the first call. To get us off to a good start, I picked someone I respected and thought would be a slam-dunk. After introducing the idea, I got this reply over the phone:

"I wouldn't buy it, Matt. If my employees are unhappy, I sack them."

After the call I turned to my co-founders, Chris and Tony, who were desperate to know how the call went. As I recounted the conversation, I saw their faces go from excited to crestfallen. Not a great start, but part of being an entrepreneur is dusting yourself off and trying again.

We continued the calls, with varying degrees of success.

FIRST MEETINGS

Chris and Tony went on to have the first face-to-face meetings. Two responses stick in their minds to this day.

A prospect to Chris Hyland: *"I loved the demo and the real-time data but there is just one problem; I don't believe in happiness."*

A prospect to Tony Latter: *"I had a meeting when a prospect walked into the room and said, 'Oh, so you're the happiness guy. Just so you know, I don't believe in happiness at work,' and at that point he left the room. In total the meeting lasted 30 seconds."*

Not the start we wanted.

However, among all the bad meetings and discouraging phone calls, we found a small group of people who instinctively believed in what we were doing. More data and research was needed for the rest, but we had enough interest to give us the confidence that we were on the right path.

"THE TIMES THEY ARE A-CHANGIN'," 2014–2018

Today, our company collects data in over 100 countries and has millions of data points on happiness. We now have customers regularly mentioning employee happiness in their board reports, ranging from global companies with over 400,000 employees to small, fast-growing, local companies with 100 or so employees. The common denominator among our customers is not size or sector, but a belief that employee happiness is important.

Next time you go for an interview, ask the interviewer, "Is employee happiness important in this company?" How and if they answer the question will tell you a lot about the company you may end up working for.

and is part of a wider ecosystem that is interdependent on many factors, including how our colleagues feel.

For years employee engagement and satisfaction surveys tried to simplify how employees feel and rationalize this data into Excel spreadsheets. The truth is that human beings are not wholly rational. We possess the ability to take a step back, reflect, and rationalize our thoughts, but that is only part of the picture.

We are emotional and instinctive beings. Understanding how thoughts and feelings interplay can be the difference between succeeding or failing as a leader.

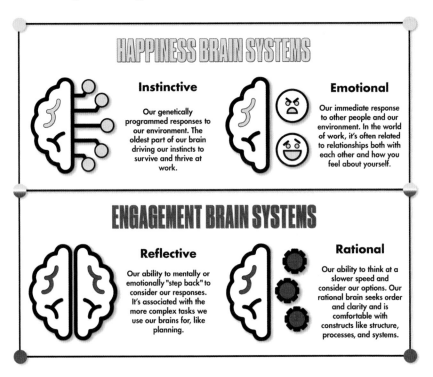

THE HAPPINESS INDEX SURVEY PROCESS

As mentioned, our Employee Engagement and Happiness Platform measures the entire employee experience, from onboarding to the day an employee leaves the organization. We gathered over 20 million data points from more than 2 million employees in over 100 countries. We also used 223,561 employee happiness and engagement research studies and 24 in-depth expert interviews. We used a deep sample of 22,000 from across the globe to visualize the data within these chapters.

When you see screenshots like this one, they are taken directly from The Happiness Index Employee Engagement and Happiness Platform.

▲ Question			Science & Technology	Food & Drinks	Public Service	Commerce	Health & Well-being
19 Meaning & Purpose			8.0	8.1	7.2	7.0	8.3	8.9
20 How inspired are you by your organization?			7.4	7.5	6.2	5.4	7.3	8.5
21 How committed are you to helping the organization succeed?			8.7	8.8	8.2	8.7	9.3	9.3

Data Collection Process

Throughout our surveys, we use a mixture of quantitative and qualitative questions. The quantitative questions gather the respondent's instinctive numerical score, which drives the insights and analytics of our platform. The qualitative questions give the respondent the opportunity to provide comments, which provide valuable context as to why they gave a particular score.

An example of the type of questions we ask is "How satisfied are you with the number of learning opportunities that are offered?" with anchor points of 1 = Very unsatisfied and 10 = Very satisfied.

The Happiness Index uses a scale of 1–10. We chose a 1–10 scale because it helps us gauge the depth behind a respondent's true drivers of engagement and happiness. On a smaller scale, such as 1–5, there is a greater perceived difference between numbers 3 and 4, whereas the broader range of a 1–10 scale gives the respondent a wider scope to be accurate in their scoring. Humans are complex with many nuances, so using a 1–10 scale allows us to see the subtle distinctions and trends that make up respondents' engagement and happiness levels.

To help respondents interpret our 1–10 scale and to remove subjectivity, our questions use anchor points such as "Never" and "Always." The anchor points sit at the start and end of the scale.

The Data and Insights

When interpreting the data and insights from a survey, we try to remove subjectivity, just like we do by using anchor points when asking questions. For example, a score of 7.6 out of 10 could mean different things to different people. Therefore, by using the following, we remove the subjectivity:

1–2 Strongly Disagree

3–4 Disagree

5–6 Neutral

7–8 Agree

9–10 Strongly Agree

When an employee is responding to a survey, we are asking them to rate their experience of the question, not how important they think that area is to their engagement and happiness. For example, rather than asking, "How important do you *feel* it is for your opinions to be listened to?" our questions are positioned as "How much do you feel your opinions are listened to?" with anchor points of 1 = Never and 10 = Always.

Tip: More information on neuroscientific methodology used by The Happiness Index can be found at https://thehappinessindex .com/books/short-reads/neuroscience-methodology/.

HAPPINESS AND ENGAGEMENT DATA

The graph seen here shows how employees were feeling in 2021. Emotions can be a strong predictor of future performance. This data could and should have helped companies prepare for the big trend of 2022, which was to become known as the *Great Resignation.* Our company, The Happiness Index, was talking about this phenomenon 12 months before everyone else, not because we are prophets of the future, but because we were looking at global happiness data in real time and separating it from employee engagement.

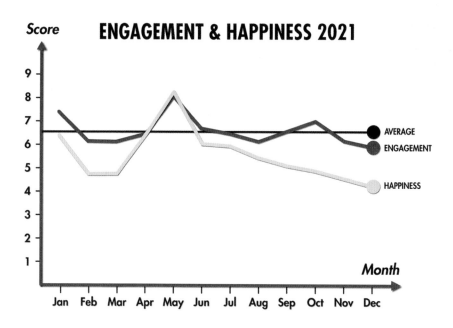

It sounds like a small change, but it is also the reason that companies that were only tracking engagement fell into a false sense of security. Engagement wasn't that far below average, but happiness was significantly lower than average.

Some HR teams who were looking at engagement data said things were okay, yet deep down in their hearts, they sensed there was a problem. They just didn't have the data to test their gut feelings and challenge their assumptions.

It was clear that employees who were not looked after during the pandemic were just sitting tight to ride out the storm. Once the opportunity came to resign, they took it. And resign they did in the millions.

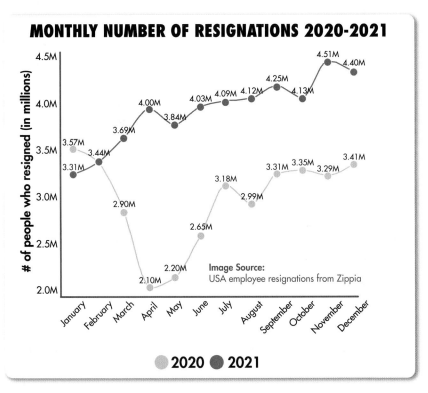

MONTHLY NUMBER OF RESIGNATIONS 2020-2021

Image Source:
USA employee resignations from Zippia

● 2020 ● 2021

Source: USA employee resignations from Zippia

The data had been there, staring us all in the face for 12 months leading up to the great resignation. However, everyone was obsessed with rational engagement data relating to how people *think*. Emotional happiness data helps us understand how people *feel*. Rational data is easier to structure, and human beings don't like unstructured data based on emotions because it can be messy.

Engagement data is an important part of the picture, but it is akin to looking at Van Gogh's famous sunflower painting and focusing only on the vase and not the 15 sunflowers sitting in it. There is way more to see when you take a step back.

Going into the pandemic, employee engagement was treated as the holy grail of the employee experience. It is useful data, but it is missing the underlying emotions about how employees are feeling. CEOs and leaders were missing the big picture.

On one hand, people say expressing emotions at work is unprofessional and belongs at home. On the other hand, these same leaders were saying they were data driven. Ignoring emotions is the opposite of being data driven. Once you see emotions as data points that help you understand the world more clearly, life and work become easier.

I found it fascinating to listen to England captain Ben Stokes reflect on England Cricket's World Cup triumph in 2022 by describing their loss in their opening game to Ireland as a catalyst for improvement:

> With that (defeat to Ireland) being so early in the competition we obviously had to address it, say what had to be said and then let it go. . . .
>
> In tournaments like these, you can't carry baggage with you, that was a little blip on the way, credit to Ireland for turning up and beating us, but the best teams learn from their mistakes and not let it affect them.

Captain Stokes and team used the experience of losing to learn and move forward. Think about a time in your career when the quality of the work you produced didn't meet your own standards. In those moments of reflection, you find ways to use that experience to improve.

PREPARING FOR CHANGE

If we know that the world—and therefore the experience of our employees—is going to change more regularly, a great starting point is to prepare for that change.

Using the brain processing model seen in the image on page 24, We updated the famous Kubler-Ross model in this change curve to help organizations navigate and understand changes, from the very small to the very large.

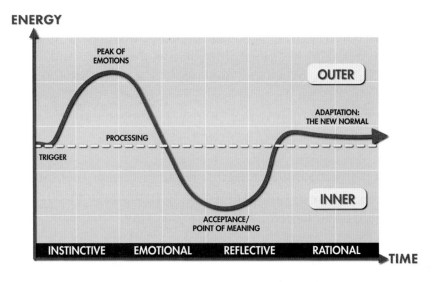

As the old saying goes, "The only constant is change." If that's true, let's prepare for it.

12 MILLION LESSONS IN HAPPINESS

In 2022, I was lucky enough to give a TEDx Talk titled "12 Million Lessons in Happiness: The super-happiness suit with inbuilt emotional deflector field." I won't ruin the TED Talk for you, but it uses data to illustrate the need to think of leadership as a nurturing role and not a command-and-control structure. It discusses the importance of emotions as a source of performance.

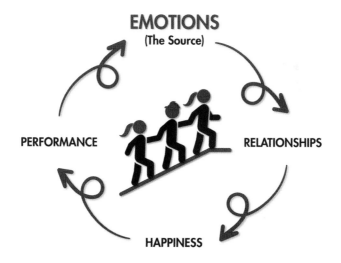

We can't control our emotions, but we can provide the right environment for our employees to thrive. We can control our actions, which is where self-control comes in, but that is very different from controlling emotions. If a colleague undermines you in a meeting, for example, it's okay to feel angry or hurt; that's a normal emotion to feel. Punching them in the face as a result of that emotion, however, is an act of losing self-control and in most countries is illegal.

When we say we control our emotions, what we really mean is that we ignore certain emotions. The emotion is still there; we just repress it. Self-control is important at work, but don't confuse that with ignoring your emotions.

As any expert gardener will explain, you can't guarantee all your plants will grow, but you *can* provide the right conditions and ingredients to give your seedlings the best chance of success. Just because some seeds fail to grow doesn't mean you should stop bothering to provide the right soil and light for the plants to have the chance to grow.

The next section looks at happiness and its impact on the *why*, *how*, and *where* we work.

WHAT'S ON EMPLOYEES' MINDS?

This Word Cloud summarizes the key subjects employees have been mentioning anonymously in The Happiness Index dataset. The next sections dive deeper into a couple of those areas as food for thought.

(2019–2023)

The Scene Is Set

The rest of this book provides the data, research, insight, and expert opinions from our guest contributors to guide you on the best conditions for employees to thrive at work.

CHAPTER 3

Employee Engagement and Happiness

In George Orwell's book *1984*, the idea of happiness is presented as meaningless. According to the infamous Big Brother, we can only survive by suppressing individual happiness and freedom. In Orwell's dystopian future, individuals are not allowed to pursue happiness because if they have freedom, they might revolt against the governing party. In modern terms, the party wanted to control how people think, feel, and behave.

In *1984*, surveillance is implemented by making people believe that they are in danger and that it is therefore essential for their safety and well-being. As lead character Winston Smith says, "Freedom is the freedom to say that two plus two makes four. If that is granted, all else follows."

Nowadays it is not just super-states that want to suppress the ideas, happiness, and creativity of individuals; organizations also attempt to do this. This relates to the misconception that productivity and employee happiness don't mix. Some organizations are consciously and unconsciously suppressing the basic human needs of their employees. This can occur in obvious ways, like distribution centers restricting toilet breaks, or law firms telling employees not to be emotional at work.

This book attempts to give individuals and organizations the insight to do their own learning and ultimately to help organizations not only survive but thrive. We call this alternative way of working the *freedom to be human*.

What Is the Freedom to Be Human?

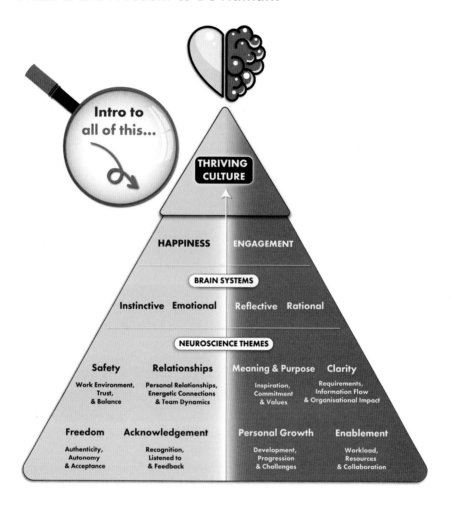

The freedom to be human is creating a culture that has all the core ingredients for employees to feel happy and engaged in their work. In our research at The Happiness Index, we discovered that, in order to thrive at work, human beings have eight universal needs: safety, relationships, meaning and purpose, clarity, freedom, acknowledgment, personal growth, and enablement.

To thrive at work, our brains need engagement and our hearts need happiness.

Happiness

Happiness relates to the instinctive and emotional processes of our brain. The *instinctive* process of the brain deals with factors like safety and freedom. The *emotional* process of the brain focuses on the factors of relationships and acknowledgment.

WHAT IS EMPLOYEE HAPPINESS?

Often, when we think of happiness, we think about mood or joy. In the workplace, this is a little simplistic. This is because mood fluctuates, and nobody's happy all the time. It was explained to me by a medical expert that being happy all the time is as much a mental health issue as being sad all the time.

When we think about happiness in the context of work, we use four neuroscience themes:

- Safety
- Relationships
- Acknowledgment
- Freedom

These neuroscience themes feed into two brain processes. The happiness-related brain processes are *instinctive* and *emotional*. This is illustrated in The Happiness Index triangle.

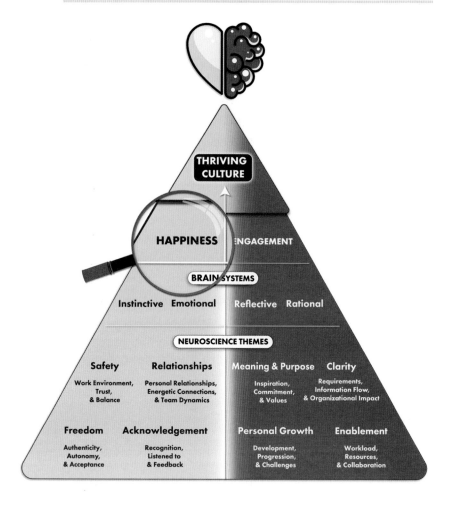

The bottom line? Creating an environment where your people feel safe and appreciated can go a long way to making them feel happier in the workplace.

WHY IS EMPLOYEE HAPPINESS IMPORTANT?

Study after study shows that happiness is linked to the bottom line. Not only are happy employees more productive, but organizations with happier employees do better in the stock market, even when other factors are controlled. On my "Happiness and Humans" podcast, Professor Alex Edmans shared this: "Companies in the United States with happier employees generated 2.3 to 3.8% higher stock returns per year than their industry peers, which is 89–184% when compounded over those 28 years."

The pandemic also had a big impact on our mental health and well-being. As we have seen, employee happiness has been impacted.

If you picked up this book because trying to create a happy working environment sounds like the morally right thing to do, that's commendable. The good news is it also makes good financial sense.

Employee Engagement

As you can see in the triangle, the engagement theme links to the reflective and rational processes of the brain. Our reflective brain looks at factors such as meaning and purpose and personal growth. The rational process of our brain deals with clarity and enablement.

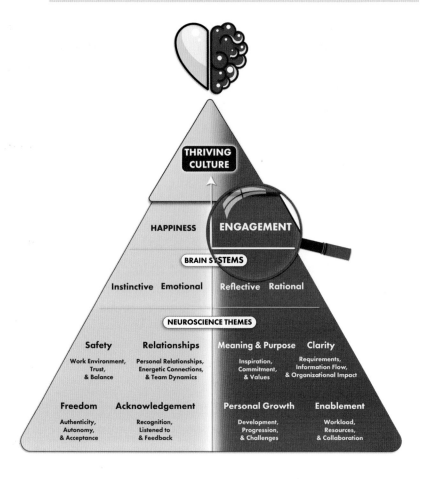

WHAT IS EMPLOYEE ENGAGEMENT?

When HR professionals talk about employee engagement, they're sometimes talking about culture and they're sometimes talking about productivity. What we mean by engagement is how connected people feel to their work.

There are four key drivers of employee engagement:

- Meaning and purpose
- Role clarity
- Personal growth
- Enablement

Depending on your team and the way they think, feel, and behave, these different factors play different roles and look different. For example, for some people, role clarity is key, and they prefer to have clearly defined areas of responsibility. Others like to be able to get involved in different projects.

There are two brain types that influence employee engagement: reflective and rational.

WHY IS EMPLOYEE ENGAGEMENT IMPORTANT?

It's hard to understate the importance of employee engagement. Engaged employees are not only likely to perform better, but they're also more likely to stay at your organization.

Attracting and retaining key talent is likely an important part of your people strategy. Many companies say their biggest asset is their people, but do they collect the data to make sure they are looking after these employees and that they feel engaged and happy? Are they providing the four drivers?

In 2018, Facebook conducted a study into their employee engagement data and found that those who stayed found their work enjoyable 31% more often, used their strengths 33% more often, and expressed 37% more confidence that they were gaining the skills and experiences they need to develop their careers.[1]

Providing clarity, purpose, personal growth, and enablement creates conditions where employees can be engaged.

Combining Employee Engagement and Happiness

So far we've talked about employee engagement and happiness and the different factors that go into creating a happy and engaged workplace. In fact, many employee engagement companies tend to:

- Lump them together
- Add a token happiness question to their engagement survey
- Rebrand engagement as happiness

I don't recommend any of these approaches—happiness and engagement need different approaches to succeed. They are also related and flow between each other.

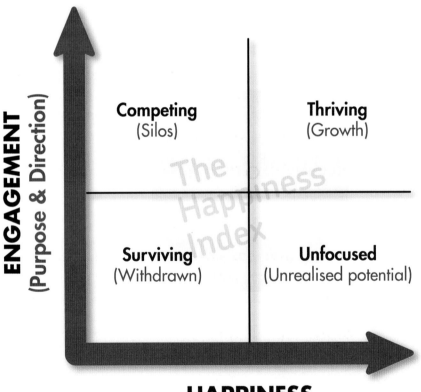

To move employees out of a competitive, unfocused and survival mode it is important to create the right conditions for both- Employee Engagement and Employee Happiness.

When you nurture these factors, they combine to create thriving workplace cultures where the people and the organisation can grow together.

Ultimately, this means you're creating the best possible environment for your team to achieve their goals. As you will learn, the different areas, or neuroscience themes, feed into brain types and then into employee engagement and happiness.

THE IMPORTANCE OF HAPPINESS AND ENGAGEMENT

Happiness and engagement are two sides of the same coin. Our brains are evolved to need both. We often talk about employee engagement and happiness as being parts of the same car. Engagement is the satnav (GPS) and happiness is the fuel. Engagement gives us direction and happiness provides energy.

It's one thing to know where you want to go; it's another to have the energy to get there.

Key Driver Analysis

This book's Key Driver Analysis looks at whether there is a relationship between these survey questions. It shows the key drivers that impact how employees feel about a given question.

This analysis helps us delve a little deeper into the wider themes because the devil is always in the details. In this dataset, the key drivers of overall employee happiness on a micro level are:

- The amount of challenge in their role (personal growth)
- How inspired they are by their organization (meaning and purpose)
- How much they trust their organization (safety)

Focusing efforts on these three specific areas is likely to have a positive impact on employee happiness.

What does healthy look like? It's some mix of safety, freedom, acknowledgment, and nurturing relationships.

Remember that it is normal and healthy for happiness levels to go up and down. But that doesn't mean that you can't improve the underlying happiness of your team over time, by providing the right environment.

Unhappy employees are more likely to be in fight, flight, or freeze mode. Creating the right conditions for employees to be happy allows them to access all those smart parts of their brains that lead to good stuff like creativity and innovation. Unhappy employees are constantly on alert and have to dedicate energy and resources to monitoring for external threats.

The insight in this book applies not only to individuals, teams, and their organizations across the world, but also to your own personal life.

This book aims to encourage organizations to create safe spaces so their employees can express how they think and feel about their work without judgment. Organizations should strive for a culture where employees can say that two plus two makes four.

The "all that else follows" in a human and organizational context is that lovely thing we call growth.

Note

1. Lori Goler, Janelle Gale, Brynn Harrington, and Adam Grant. "Why people really quit their jobs," *Harvard Business Review,* https://hbr.org/2018/01/why-people-really-quit-their-jobs

CHAPTER 4

Emotions as Data Points

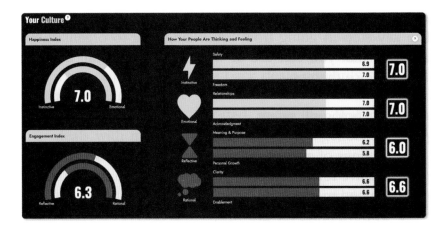

Before we go into the data in the eight neuroscience chapters, let's look at what we mean by instinctive, emotional, reflective, and rational data systems.

Instinctive Data

Instinctive data is concerned primarily with two needs, commonly referred to as "survive" and "thrive." Our genetic programming gives us the basic instructions we need to survive. We are constantly on the lookout for any threat that jeopardizes our survival. This is of course essential to the longevity of the human species, but in an organizational context, it has a downside. People in survival mode cannot give their best, because their brains remain focused primarily on addressing ongoing threats.

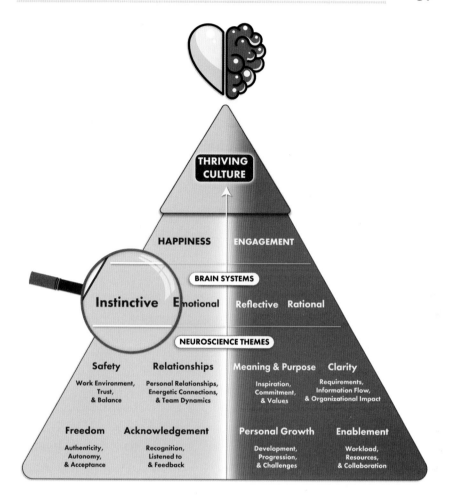

The consequence is that these people operate at a suboptimal level. To perform at our best, we need to feel safe. This allows energy to be available for more constructive, collaborative, and creative activities. This is why it is important to understand how safe people feel.

Our instincts are not just concerned with survival, however. We also have a genetic need to thrive and to extend our boundaries of influence. The human species is innately curious and exploratory, and this sits at the heart of our evolutionary momentum. To give our best, we need the freedom to be ourselves and to be able to explore our environments.

Q1. What Characteristics Are My Team Members Likely to Show When in Instinctive Mode?

The main source of motivation for teams that are in instinctive mode is *delivering results*. Team members tend to demonstrate the following characteristics:

- Direct
- Result focused
- Challenging
- Competitive
- Driven
- Self-starter
- Firm

Q2. How Can I Help My Team Members Be Instinctive?

Consider these questions:

- Could improvements be made to the physical environment?
- Is there an adequate level of trust? What can you do to boost this?
- Do your people feel there is a fair balance between work and home life?
- Are people able to be their true selves at work? If not, what could you recommend?
- Do people feel they have the freedom in their roles to explore, or are they being micromanaged?

Q3. What Does the Instinctive Style Bring to a Team and What Type of Environment Suits It?

Teams that have an instinctive style tend to have the following characteristics:

- Organization
- Challenge each other in a safe way
- Get things done
- Make decisions
- Demand results
- Uncompromising
- Compelling
- Confident

They tend to thrive in environments where:

- They have freedom.
- Results are prioritized.
- Their work is nonroutine.
- They work with challenges and opportunities.

Q4. How Do I Best Work with a Team in Instinctive Mode?

Avoid
- Going into too much detail
- Overly focusing on feelings or future challenges
- Telling them what to do

Try
- Getting to the point
- Being conclusive
- Presenting solutions, not problems
- Empowering them to make decisions
- Showing independence

In terms of personal growth, employees need to feel they are learning and developing. The work they do needs to stretch and energize them and the organization needs to offer opportunities for career development and progression. Moreover, people want to feel inspired by their work. They seek meaningful activity with a clear and fulfilling purpose.

Q1. What Characteristics Are My Team Members Likely to Show If They Are in Reflective Mode?
The main source of motivation for teams with a reflective style is deriving meaning from their work. They tend to demonstrate the following characteristics:

- Visionary
- Flexible
- Thoughtful
- Insightful
- Intuitive
- Accommodating
- Open minded

Q2. How Do I Help My Team Members Be Reflective?
Consider these questions:

- Can you provide more training and development opportunities?
- Are there career progression pathways? If not, can you introduce them?
- If employees are not feeling challenged in their roles, how can you introduce this?
- To help inspire your people, do you need to recommunicate your vision?
- Can you create opportunities in the year for individuals and teams to reflect on and share what they have learned?

Q3. What Does a Reflective Style Bring to a Team and What Type of Environment Suits This Style?

Teams in reflective mode tend to have the following characteristics:

- Vision: They see the bigger picture.
- They often provide a different insight.
- They tend toward open mindedness.
- They demonstrate intuitive thinking.

They tend to thrive in environments where:

- They are free from restrictive rules.
- There is little conflict.
- They have the time for reflection.
- There is a forum to discuss their insights or vision.

Q4. How Do I Best Work with a Team in Reflective Mode?

Avoid
- Forcing quick decisions
- Being overly opinionated
- Ignoring potential consequences

Try
- Painting a picture of the future
- Avoiding direct conflict
- Allowing time for reflection
- Keeping an open mind
- Framing your points using different perspectives

In all cases, these themes run deep within the processing of the human brain and have significant impact on our behavior and life experiences. Once the challenges have been fully explored and agreed upon, a suitable response plan needs to be put in place, one that is created collaboratively and is most likely to secure the commitment of those involved.

Rational Thought

Human capacity for rational thought is far more advanced than in any other living species and this is reflected in the size and sophistication of the human cortex. Rational thought is concerned with interpretation and execution, and ultimately with getting things done. Its role is essentially practical. We have the capacity for action at a more basic instinctive level, but this is where we establish the rules of execution for the complex capabilities we learn through life.

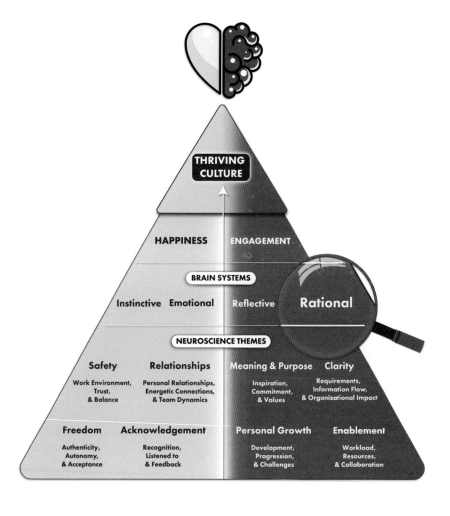

We need to be clear about all sorts of relevant factors to be able to take appropriate and effective action. The neural pathways we create in our brains are our rules of engagement. To perform at our best, we need clarity on such matters as what is expected of us, what outcomes we are expected to achieve, what authority we have, who we are expected to engage with, what information we have access to, and so on. We therefore focus our questions on requirements, information flow, and organizational impact.

We then need to have the means to get the job done. While clarity focuses on the "what," enablement focuses on the "how." Hence our questions focus on workload, resources, and collaboration opportunities.

Q1. What Characteristics Are My Team Members Likely to Show If They Are in Rational Mode?

Teams in rational mode tend to demonstrate the following characteristics:

- Precise
- Systematic
- Analytical
- Diligent
- Reliable
- Methodical
- Objective

Q2. How Do I Help My Team Members Be Rational?

The main source of motivation for teams operating in the rational style is having clarity in what they can deliver. Consider these questions:

- Are employees clear on what they need to do? Reinforcing job roles and responsibilities will help with this.
- If employees do not feel informed, revisit your communication strategy.

extensive. As a global population the employee workforce is diverse and balanced, but most organizations tend to score highly in some areas and low in others.

For example, a company led by a rational leadership team might not be providing enough employee recognition, meaning that acknowledgment is low and the emotional needs of the employees are not being met. On the other hand, a company led by an emotional leadership team might not be providing enough information flow for employees to get clarity and meet their rational needs.

Summary

Now that we've explored brain data and systems, it's time to look at some of the implications of this in the everyday experiences of people working in organizations.

The next eight chapters discuss the eight themes recognized and identified as indicative of the four natural brain states in this model that sit within the instinctive, emotional, rational, and reflective data systems.

As a quick reminder, those eight themes are:

- Safety (Instinctive)
- Freedom (Instinctive)
- Clarity (Rational)
- Enablement (Rational)
- Relationships (Emotional)
- Acknowledgment (Emotional)
- Meaning and purpose (Reflective)
- Opportunities for growth (Reflective)

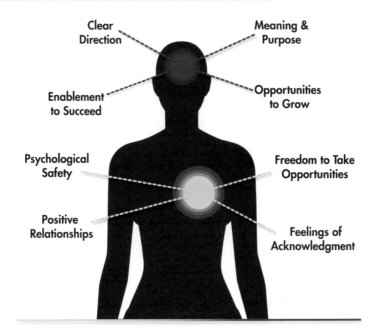

Before starting the next chapter, try arranging these themes in order of importance in your own head. Consider sending this list to your team and asking them to do the same. I do this with all my teams. It is fascinating to see the diversity of answers and it creates great empathy within a team about what is important to them.

The first area we'll discuss is psychological safety.

CHAPTER 5

Psychological Safety

Team psychological safety is a shared belief that people feel safe about the interpersonal risks that arise concerning their behaviors in a team context.[2]

Across our database, safety is one of the lowest-scoring neuroscience themes (7.5). This is primarily driven by a lower score given to work–life balance (7.2). This indicates that organizations need to focus on improving the work–life balance needs of their employees if they want to improve psychological safety.

By analyzing the study's comments relating to work–life balance, we can conclude that employees often feel they have to choose between work and private life. Consider these specific insights from our study:

- **Customer Insight 1:** "Change impacts stability, which impacts uncertainty, which impacts safety, which impacts trust. Tracking the changes in how people feel allowed us to maintain psychological safety and trust levels."
- **Customer Insight 2:** "The data indicated that the majority of their people wanted to go back to the office when lockdown eased, so they opened their office with all the necessary safety measures for those who wanted to return. However, the data also indicated their people were fearful of public transport, so they started exploring ways of easing this concern, like flexible start times."
- **Customer Insight 3:** "By listening to employee voices in real time, we were able to calm individual fears about health and safety concerns about a particular site. Physical safety concerns were resulting in poor psychological safety and were eroding trust. In reality, they had a communications issue, not a safety issue, but the data helped them identify the problem and fix it."

Lowest Scoring Factors	Av. Rating
Opportunities to progress (Personal Growth)	6.8
Opinions listened to (Acknowledgment)	7.1
Training (Personal Growth)	7.2
Work and home-life balance (Safety)	7.2

The Impact of Psychological Safety on Performance, Innovation, and Creativity

Google launched a research project called Project Aristotle, which explored over 250 team-level variables. They found that successful Google teams have five elements in common: psychological safety, dependability, structure and clarity, meaning, and impact of work. Of these factors, psychological safety was found to be the most important factor in successful teams.[3]

Singh and colleagues[4] found that, as well as directly and strongly influencing performance at the individual and team levels, psychological safety has been found to influence performance indirectly through facilitating learning behavior at both the individual and team levels.

Within psychological safety, this chapter drills down into three subareas:

- Work environment
- Work–life harmony
- Trust

WORK ENVIRONMENT

People need to feel that their physical working environment is safe, that it poses no danger in terms of conditions or access. This includes emotional safety, such as freedom from bullying, prejudice, or psychological abuse and harassment.

Some organisations naturally understand the importance of the working environment by offering basic working conditions like flexible working. However some organisations are struggling to evolve with the new world and offer stubbornly rigid employee experiences and working conditions.

My belief is that ultimately stubborn organisations resistant to change will lose out in the war for talent. Companies that evolve will attract and retain the best talent and therefore outperform their peers in the long term.

Creating a better employee experience than your competitors is a simple route to competitive advantage in the marketplace.

Overall, I believe the "where you work" debate has been a distraction from the more important "command and control" conversation.

Some companies require employees to work from physical locations yet treat their employees really well, giving them some autonomy and trust. There are organizations who allow their employees to work from home but track every single keystroke and monitor how much time they spend away from their desks in their own homes.

What I believe is that some employees prefer to work from the office and some employees prefer to work from home—but *all* employees want flexibility.

Flexibility means different things to different employees in different roles. Flexibility for a security guard in a supermarket might mean being able to swap shifts with a colleague without needing to check with the supervisor 400 times.

Flexibility for an army veteran now working in an office could be being able to work from home when their PTSD is getting on top of them and the commute on the train on that particular day is causing extreme anxiety.

External Research

For me, the physical environment is where you do your work and becomes easier to visualize when you think of it as your "work home," as opposed to "the office," which can bring up images of Ricky Gervais's award-winning sitcom.

Your work home might be a remote location or it might be in a city cafe, but once you start thinking of it as your work home, things become simpler. Human beings need a home. That is true even if you work 100% virtually.

In our first company, 4Ps, we added a playroom for children to our London office to help parents with childcare. To this day, it was one of the best moves we ever made. It made that place we called an office more like a home.

It was a home where we did our work, but a much more human one. I never did the math, but I can guarantee you the return on investment was positive when I looked at better employee retention, greater understanding between parents and non-parents, and appreciation from customers who wanted to work with us because they could see we were trying to treat our employees well. We don't always get the employee experience of our employees right, but we do try.

There is now more research into the impact of the natural world and nature on our work. Stephen and Rachel Kaplan found:

> Proponents of introducing greenery to the workplace argue that natural environments restore people's capacity for directed attention, whereas built environments tend to deplete this capacity. Natural environments exert less demand on directed attention and encourage more effortless brain functions, thereby allowing the capacity for attention to be restored.
>
> Thus, after an interaction with natural environments, one is able to perform better on tasks that rely on directed attention such as data crunching or complex problem solving. According to this

view, plants in the workplace should enhance employees' directed-attention capacity and therefore enhance their concentration and productivity levels.[5]

WORK-LIFE HARMONY

With people carrying a phone in their pockets with more computing power than the first spaceship that carried humanity to the moon, it can often be hard to balance our work and our private lives.

Work–life harmony covers whether people feel that they are in a state of reasonable balance in terms of juggling their work and personal/family commitments and emotional needs. Excessive work pressure will cause difficulties in personal relationships and will limit people's capacity to recover their energy.

External Research

In 2022, there was some really interesting research and the first of its kind, focused on the work–life balance of female construction professionals in the Nigerian construction industry.

The research by L. O. Oyewobi and colleagues found that work–life policies enable employees to balance their work and family responsibilities, which in turn increases organizational commitment.[6]

Expert View

"Work–life balance is in the lowest 10% of factors in The Happiness Index dataset, which is an indication that there's a lot of work that organizations need to do here. Focus and policy in this area can positively move the dial for all employees, whatever their background."

—Laura Page, The Happiness Index

Every time, we started at zero trust with the new CEO. These times were really challenging for us personally, but more importantly there was a knock-on impact on our employees' happiness that we could see in the data.

Things came to a head in a meeting when a senior leader in the parent company uttered the following words to me and my co-founder Chris Hyland, which will be etched in my soul for eternity: "The thing is, culture does not really matter."

At this exact moment, I decided I had to leave the company I had co-founded ten years earlier. Within three months, we had negotiated our exit. I spent the summer with my young children watching the World Cup.

Why Is Psychological Safety So Important?

If we feel unsafe, our brains are in survival mode. This has a material impact on our emotions and on our ability to engage and perform. Effectively, we are only using the parts of our brain needed to help us survive. Consequently, we struggle to access our own talents that are crucial to our ongoing success, such as seeing the bigger picture, committing to the team, being creative, retaining objectivity and perspective, and thinking clearly. The list goes on.

In survival mode, we offer our organization the bare minimum we need to keep our jobs, which means superficial compliance rather than genuine commitment. This applies most obviously to matters of physical safety, but also to working in an atmosphere of mistrust, or feeling that the expectations placed on our workload are unrealistic. Each of these holds back—the individual and the organization.

How Can Organizations Respond?

When we have data telling us that employees feel unsafe, we need to explore what the perceived threats are. This should be done collaboratively. Study where possible the threats can be removed or at least reduced. In some cases, the threats may be an issue of perception rather than reality, but that does not make them any less potent. Organizational perception needs to be handled with sensitivity, integrity, and honesty. Lack of trust is a big issue in many organizations. The opportunity cost associated with an untrusting culture is enormous.

Summary

Once your team instinctively feels safe, you can move to the second instinctive theme—freedom.

When I list the eight themes in order of importance in my own life, freedom comes out on top every time.

Notes

1. https://www.sciencedirect.com/science/article/pii/S10 53482217300013
2. A.C. Edmondson, *The Fearless Organization: Creating Psychological Safety in the Workplace for Learning, Innovation, and Growth* (Hoboken, NJ: John Wiley & Sons).
3. Julia Rozovsky, "Project Aristotle: The five keys to a successful Google team," November 2015, https://rework .withgoogle.com/blog/five-keys-to-a-successful-google-team/
4. B. Singh et al., "Managing diversity at work: Does psychological safety hold the key to racial differences in employee performance?" https://doi/10.1111/joop.12015
5. S. Kaplan and R. Kaplan, *Humanscape: Environments for People* (University of Michigan, 1982), cited in Kaushal Modi and Sangramsinh Parmar, "Understanding biophilia

and its integration with architecture," *International Journal of Scientific & Engineering Research* 11 (no. 5, 2020), https://www.researchgate.net/profile/Sangramsinh-Parmar-2/publication/343190808_Understanding_Biophilia_and_its_integration_with_Architecture/links/5f1b106a92851cd5fa42a12b/Understanding-Biophilia-and-its-integration-with-Architecture.pdf.

6. L.O. Oyewobi, A.E. Oke, T.D. Adeneye, A.R. Jimoh, and A.O. Windapo, "Impact of work–life policies on organizational commitment of construction professionals: Role of work–life balance," https://doi.org/10.1080/15623599.2020.1742632

7. Mohammad Babamiri, Ziba Abdi, and Nasrin Noori, "Investigating the factors that influence Iranian nurses' workplace happiness," https://journals.rcni.com/nursing-management/evidence-and-practice/investigating-the-factors-that-influence-iranian-nurses-workplace-happiness-nm.2021.e1972/abs

CHAPTER 6

Freedom

As an entrepreneur, I find freedom incredibly important, as it is for all human beings. The more you understand your employees and how they rank these areas in importance, the easier it is to work with them and motivate them.

One person on my team says that freedom is their number-one driver and another team member says clarity is the most important driver for them.

For the person who says freedom is their number-one driver, a daily call with them might feel like micromanagement. This person prefers a monthly check-in meeting.

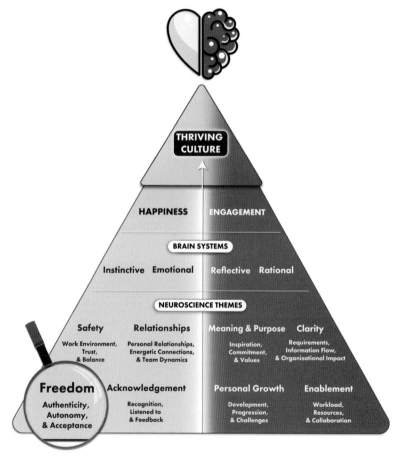

For the person on my team who says that clarity is number one, checking in with them only once a month would feel like I don't care. A short check-in a few times a week helps them feel on track and cared for.

If even identical twins have different personalities (as studies show), it makes sense that we need to adapt our leadership approach on an employee-by-employee basis. Some people worry that this approach will take more time, and it does initially. But the time you save having happy and engaged employees easily offsets this small investment of time.

Defining Freedom at Work

Freedom at work is the ability, as far as possible, to choose your own path.

The neuroscience theme of freedom generally scores well (7.9), indicating that employees in the study generally felt that they had the freedom they needed to do their jobs.

However, when analyzing the insight by sectors, it becomes clear that freedom is not universal. For example, the public service sector (such as law enforcement, military service, and public health) scored 6.8, which is significantly less than the mean (7.9). The insight shows that employees in public service organizations do not feel they are "free to be their true selves at work" and have lower levels of autonomy to perform their role.

Consider these specific insights from our study:

- **Customer Insight 1:** "We had one customer who wanted to take well-being more seriously, so created a one-hour slot in the day that was ring fenced and employees were encouraged to do something that was good for their well-being. Although this idea came from a good place, with good intentions, it caused friction; some employees described it as "enforced" breaks. It is another example that employees want freedom to choose the way that works best for them."

- **Customer Insight 2:** "Many of our customers have launched new flexible working policies and used data to help design them. Data has focused organizations on what people want from flexible working. This cultural intelligence has helped make changes in areas that have real-life impacts. For example, data from our customer shows that when flexible working is introduced for working parents, it removes stress and worry, which is replaced with freedom and trust."

▲ Question			Science & Technology	Food & Drinks	Public Service
5	Freedom		7.6	8.0	7.4	6.8
6	How free do you feel to be your true self at work?		7.6	7.9	7.6	7.0
7	How satisfied are you with the level of freedom you have in your role?		7.6	8.0	7.2	6.8

Within freedom, this chapter drills down into three subareas:

- Acceptance and belonging
- Authenticity
- Autonomy

Notes

1. J. Andrew Elliot, *Advances in Motivation Science* (Elsevier, 2022).
2. Anantha Raj A. Arokiasamy, Hanif Rizaldy, and Ranfeng Qiu, "Exploring the impact of authentic leadership and work engagement on turnover intention: The moderating role of job satisfaction and organizational size," *Advances in Decision Sciences; Taichung* 26 (no. 2, June 2022): 1–21, https://www.proquest.com/openview/0ab481763bcb10ed a7635d216beceb6b/1?pq-origsite=gscholar&cbl=25336
3. Fayaz A. Soomro, Dr. Sadaf Khan, Jehanzeb Khan, Wajid Mehmood, and Farman Ullah Jan. "Impact of emotional intelligence on job autonomy," *Journal of Contemporary Issues in Business and Government* 28(3): 299–317. doi: 10.47750/cibg. https://cibgp.com/article_17608.html

CHAPTER 7

Feelings of Acknowledgment

In The Happiness Index dataset, acknowledgment is the area with the widest range of responses. What this means is that not only is acknowledgment incredibly important, but the way people want to be acknowledged varies greatly from person to person.

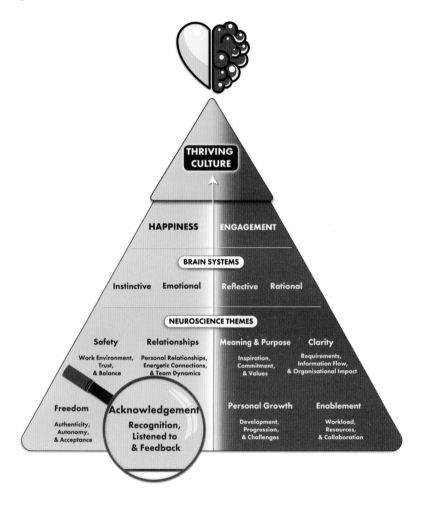

One of your team may really appreciate being acknowledged at the all-company meeting, but for another employee this type of acknowledgment may be their worst nightmare and could cause embarrassment.

I made this mistake personally when I gave one of our senior engineers a shoutout for great work on the upgrade of our employee engagement and happiness platform in the all-company meeting. My intention was to say thank you, but I got it wrong. I accidentally put someone in a situation that made them feel uncomfortable. Instead, I should have taken that person for a quiet coffee and said thank you privately.

We are all learning all the time. I try to turn my mistakes into learning opportunities. Once again, knowing your team and what makes them tick is key.

What Are Feelings of Acknowledgment?

Acknowledgment is a feeling of emotional validation of who we are and what we are experiencing—the feeling of being heard. It is one of the most important human needs. We see organizations regularly falling short in this area.

Acknowledgment is the joint lowest-scoring theme (7.2). This indicates that employees are not feeling comparatively acknowledged doing their jobs; a further deep-dive into why is important.

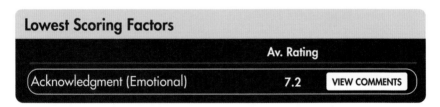

Lowest Scoring Factors		
	Av. Rating	
Acknowledgment (Emotional)	7.2	VIEW COMMENTS

The reason for this is that employees do not feel they are "listened to" and, as a result, do not feel "valued as an individual." If the acknowledgment needs of employees continue to be unfulfilled, this can result in a lack of connection with the organization. Many employees end up feeling that they are not contributing and are unproductive.

Consider these specific insights from our study:

- **Customer Insight 1:** "The manager/non-manager paradox: Managers tend to score more positively than non-managers. This is due to various reasons, including recognition, feeling closer to the vision, and more experience that has led to greater confidence and remuneration."
- **Customer Insight 2:** "Recognition delivered in the wrong way can demotivate employees. A shoutout was made for a manager who is a single parent and was praised for working late at night and weekends to maintain performance. The inference was that everybody should be doing the same, even if it's not mentally or physically possible for everyone. People are striving to perform as best they can but this attitude leaves people feeling inadequate."

Within acknowledgment, this chapter drills down into three subareas:

- Feeling listened to
- Being recognized
- Getting feedback

FEELING LISTENED TO

When we express a thought or feeling, it is important to us that our views are heard. This is a subtle yet critical experience that helps us understand our impact on the world. Not being listened to is a form of sensory deprivation that is emotionally destabilizing. It can make us feel unsure about who we are and whether we are important.

External Research

Emma Nordbäck, a researcher and professor, found that there was a validation impact on having an internal coach trained in active listening in a Finnish engineering company:

> An employee in need of validation viewed a peer coach as "an ear" that listened to those thoughts and feelings on a regular basis, or as "a shoulder to lean on," who offered emotional support.
>
> Those employees valued a coach who engaged in active listening, and did indeed help affirm the coachee's thoughts and feelings. As a result of this function, coachees commonly perceived that they gained peace of mind, a feeling of being socially connected, and of becoming emotionally recharged.[1]

BEING RECOGNIZED

Recognition informs us that we are doing things right, which in turn gives us a sense of emotional validation. This is not limited to formalized recognition schemes and rewards, but is the much wider and richer tapestry of human-to-human acknowledgment expressed at an authentic interpersonal level.

External Research

A report produced by the Society of Human Resource Management found that "51 percent of supervisors stated they recognize employees who do a good job; however, only 17 percent of the employees at the same organizations reported that their supervisors recognize them sufficiently."[2]

This gap illustrates the importance of speaking to your team and understanding them. As with my mistake discussed at the beginning of the chapter, over half of these managers felt they were recognizing their employees, but only 17% of employees felt that they had actually been recognized. I can do better; we can all do better in this area.

According to a recent survey conducted by the *Chicago Tribune* of over 30,000 individuals, the number-one reason cited by employees who enjoy their work was "I feel genuinely appreciated at this company."[3] I love this finding because it shows how simple and free of charge this area is. Human beings just want to feel appreciated.

Moving away from the research for a moment to focus on my friendship groups, I have heard more and more of my friends say that work just feels a bit more transactional these days. Many of my close friends now work virtually and appreciation in a virtual world is a skill set of its own. I am not saying it can't be done well, but the world of work as we know it has had decades of perfecting the art of appreciation in the physical world and only a few years of recognizing our employees virtually.

We will get better at this, and I encourage you to keep testing and learning in this area. Ask your employees about this subject and make them part of the solution. Try not to fall into the trap of recognition becoming transactional or you will defeat the purpose. For example, if you automate an email to go out to your team every Friday at 4 p.m. thanking them for their work, that would be a terrible idea and not very "heartfelt."

The important word here is *heartfelt*. Other human beings need to feel that your words come from the heart.

Expert View

"Every single human being is different and recognition is never the same for two people. Don't underestimate the role that relationships and emotions play in recognition. You can think you are doing recognition really well, but if you have not done your homework on an individual's needs, you could be getting it completely wrong."

—Simon Berry, Recognition Expert

GETTING FEEDBACK

I remember the first time I heard someone say, "Feedback is a gift." I almost vomited in my own mouth. Not that the statement isn't true but it felt like a cliché too far. Feedback may be a gift, but most of us are pretty rubbish at giving and receiving feedback.

Regular feedback is a vital component of emotional sustainability and growth. Receiving timely and relevant levels of feedback, delivered with appropriate skill and care, can be a critical personal development opportunity, helping people to keep on track on their own meaningful journeys.

External Research

Filipa Castanheira and her colleagues wrote a paper called "The role of reaction to feedback in the relationship between performance management, job satisfaction and the leader–member exchange."[4] The quantitative study collected data by questionnaire, with participation from 1,815 workers from a customer service company in Portugal. Three effects were observed in this study:

- Performance management is an important part of the reaction to feedback and of the supervisor–employee relationship.
- Reaction to feedback fully mediated the effect of performance management on job satisfaction.
- Reaction to feedback partially mediated the effect of the performance management on the supervisor–employee relationship.

Filipa also found that it is important to consider how positively you deliver constructive feedback:

> Our research suggests that the individual characteristics of the leader play an important role in providing, through feedback, the valuable content that fosters information processing. A high degree

of agreeableness in a leader influences the emotional tone of their feedback. The emotional tone is interpreted as an informational signal by the receiving team, muting the effectiveness of the other tactical information present in the constructive feedback.

I don't take this research to mean we need to be rough with our feedback, but it is a reminder not to present constructive feedback in an overly positive light. For example, if you need to tell someone that their behavior is being perceived as bullying, it's important to deliver the feedback in a way that doesn't trivialize the message.

This is another great reason that we need to practice giving and receiving feedback, so it feels like a normal part of work and not like having your tooth extracted on Christmas Eve (like my son Fred had to endure in 2021—not a pretty sight, poor little fella). Feedback should not feel like undergoing dental work.

Expert View

"All feedback is not equal. It is important to consider the source of the feedback. Self-awareness is incredibly important for feedback. Feedback needs to be specific, and remember to ask for consent before offering feedback where appropriate."

—Karen Robinson, Founding Director of The Flockist

Why Are Feelings of Acknowledgment So Important?

The need for acknowledgment runs deep. We have very sophisticated sensory systems seeking out information about how we are impacting people around us at an emotional level. This enables us to constantly refresh our behavior and to make

CHAPTER **8**

Positive Relationships

As a group of factors, relationships consistently rank at the top of almost every country in the 100-plus in which we collect data. It is yet another beautiful reminder that human beings are social animals.

It is also important not to let the introvert-extrovert debate distract us here. If someone doesn't want to go to the all-hands company party because they don't like big group gatherings, that doesn't mean they don't care about relationships or don't want to have positive relationships with their colleagues. It just means they want to interact in a different way. It is a leader's job to find out the best way to do this.

Some leaders found success in their careers because they thrive in large social settings, but that doesn't mean it's the same for everyone. How you nurture positive relationships among your team will be key to creating conditions where the underlying happiness of your employees can improve.

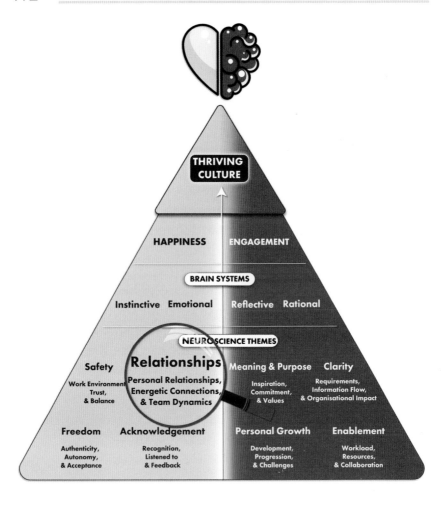

It is also worth pointing out that relationships need to be authentic; otherwise they will break down at the first sign of trouble. In any relationship, if you only ever discuss the good stuff and avoid the tough conversations, then that relationship will struggle once you hit a bit of choppy water.

Positive relationships are for all weathers and economic backdrops.

What Are Positive Relationships?

Positive relationships are the experience of working relationships that sustain us emotionally.

In The Happiness Index study, relationships is our highest-scoring theme, with a score of 8.5 out of 10, indicating the employees had strong positive relationships with their coworkers. All three questions on this topic scored well with employees across the globe. As we know, relationships are key to creating energy. The main drivers of this high score were positive responses to "Enjoying working with your team" (8.5) and "Positive relationships" (8.3).

Consider these specific insights from our study:

- **Customer Insight 1:** "Even in organizations where rela-tionships are strong, we still see a drop-off when it comes to relationships between different teams. Silo working is prevalent in almost all our datasets and is an area organizations can quickly improve on by digging a little deeper into their data."
- **Customer Insight 2:** "Personality type is not something that many HR policies consider. One of our customers wrote this to us and it really makes you think: 'In terms of gender and sexuality, I feel very safe to express myself. However, personality-wise, I feel I need to accommodate for the professional environment.'"

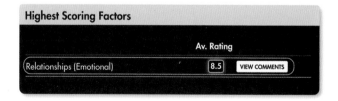

As you can see and no doubt feel yourself, positive relationships with colleagues are a vital source of emotional nourishment. These are the people we spend the most time with at work and who therefore have a significant influence on our daily experience, offering comfort and support, discomfort or rejection.

Within relationships, this chapter drills down into three subareas:

- Energetic connections
- Personal relationships
- Team dynamics and management style

ENERGETIC CONNECTIONS

Feeling energetically connected to our colleagues is that sense of understanding each other. You are on the same wavelength and naturally click.

In the calmer state, this is empathy, and when we are energized, this can become a team that would describe themselves with terms such as "buzzing" or "alive," a natural unforced state of understanding, togetherness, and bonding.

External Research

If you enjoyed my colleague Clive Hyland's book *The Quantum Way: Understanding the Science Behind Happiness and Workplace Engagement,* you may have also noticed that three scientists just won the Nobel prize for their work on quantum mechanics: John F. Clauser, Anton Zeilinger, and Alain Aspect.

Physics.org said about their Nobel Prize in Physics 2022:

> They demonstrated that unseen particles, such as photons, can be linked, or "entangled," with each other even when they are separated by large distances. . . .What the work shows is "parts of the universe—even those at great distances from each other—are connected. . . .Quantum information "has broad and potential implications in areas such as secure information transfer, quantum computing, and sensing technology," said Eva Olsson, a member of the Nobel committee.[1]

I am not about to go into a quantum physics lecture, mainly because I am not smart enough, but it is worth sharing that the reason we use quantum research to aid our understanding of work is because, at a fundamental level, we are all energy. Once you start thinking about yourself and your colleagues as energy, it leads to understanding the importance of energetic connections. The research in this area is mind boggling and I do expect further research from the quantum world to aid our understanding of the world of work.

Before you start thinking human beings are super-smart and invented things like flight and blockchains, this is yet more evidence that everything we think we have invented has probably already been perfected by either nature in terms of flight (see the bumble bee) or the universe's version of a blockchain that we now call entanglement.

My favorite learning from quantum physics will always be this famous quote from Richard Feynman: "If you think you understand quantum mechanics, then you don't."

PERSONAL RELATIONSHIPS

This continues with the theme that there is a particular dynamic around teamwork that can give us a sense of community and collective bonding. Being able to connect with a team provides a vital social ingredient to our emotional needs and gives us the opportunity to feel that we belong.

External Research

The most interesting research in this area is the view that personal relationships work like a multiplier for all other areas of the business, like some super-booster.

Denise M. Rousseau and Kimberly Ling state, "Positive relationships substantially multiply the potentialities of people and organizations." They also go one step further to explain that they are generative in nature too: "Having the power to originate and propagate something that would not exist otherwise."[2]

Wow—just wow. Both those points clearly illustrate how important relationships are to success.

Let's now take a look at relationships from a community perspective. A focus on positive community in research by Ruth Blatt and Carl Camden and by Kathleen McGinn illustrates how "short-term connections as well as long-term, institutionalized connections can be transformed in feeling and function by patterns of positive interactions and the structures that shape and sustain interaction."[3,4]

I see this as a good reminder that employee and customer experiences—even with people they might not meet again—is incredibly important. Think about the freelance receptionist who welcomes your biggest customer or the external recruiter who makes the first call to the new CEO you are trying to headhunt. These might seem like small interactions, but they can have both negative and positive outcomes and it's helpful to see them as an important part of the wider work experience.

I remember having a terrible experience at a global headquarters in London a few years back. I was not welcomed by the person at reception. When I discussed it with my contact, they said the person who was rude was simply a temp. That may have been true, but that temp had a big impact on my experience and how I felt for the rest of that afternoon.

There is also research showing the importance of developmental networks by Hannah Higgins and Douglas Kahn[5] and Belle Ragins and Amy Verbos[6] that looks at how people inside and outside of an organization's boundaries are connected to one another in ways that create growth, development, authenticity, and successful performance on the job.

When we set out to measure employee happiness, we were also looking at customer happiness. It is important to consider, for example, how a toxic customer could be impacting your internal culture.

We have fired a few customers over the years and in my experience down the line the long-term positive impact always outweighs the short-term financial loss. Easier said than done when the finance director is giving you a hard time about the quarterly retention numbers, but don't be afraid to call it a day with that toxic customer who treats your employees badly. The energy drain of toxic relationships can be huge on a team. Sometimes you don't realize until things change and you have a release of new positive energy.

At this point I also want to point out the danger of identifying individuals as toxic before you have provided the right environmental conditions. Stress can do strange things to people and it is our responsibility to fix the culture so all employees from all backgrounds can thrive.

I loved Jemma Maclean's Human Horticulture Disrupt HR presentation[7] and specifically this quote: "Caring for a cactus is going to be very different to caring for a marigold," which puts it all nicely into context for me.

Expert View

"Be intentional with personal relationships and practice getting better at them."

—Cathy Courtenay, Delivering Happiness

I loved Cathy's point here in my "Happiness and Humans" podcast interview, because it's a reminder that relationships need to be valued and we need to work hard at them.

TEAM DYNAMICS AND MANAGEMENT STYLE

As the saying goes, "People don't leave bad companies, they leave a bad manager," or something like that.

"Line manager" might sound like an outdated term these days, but no matter how flat your internal org chart is, there will be some kind of power dynamic in play, and these relationships will impact the happiness of your employees.

Sometimes people tell me they have no hierarchy or power structures but then I remind them they pay their employees and that pay is one of the strongest power dynamics. For example, you might have the power to control whether your employee can pay their rent or mortgage.

The relationship between worker and immediate manager is always important, even if you have evolved to a modern coaching style of leadership. This relationship has a substantial impact on the employee's daily experience and can set the conditions for emotional success or failure.

External Research

Kerstin Alfes, Catherine Truss, and colleagues did two super-interesting studies in this area:

> Two studies with a total of 1,796 participants were conducted in service-sector organizations in the United Kingdom and analyzed using structural equation modeling. The data reveal that perceived line manager behavior and perceived HR practices are linked with employee engagement.
>
> In turn, employee engagement is strongly linked to individual performance and fully mediates the link between both perceived HR practices and perceived line manager behavior and self-report task performance as well as self-report innovative work behavior. The findings show the significance of the line manager in the HR-performance link, and the mediating role played by employee engagement.[8]

Expert View

"Managers who are only looking at who is delivering things that can be measured in outputs will struggle in this area. For example, we should value people who are really good at learning outside of what they already know. If you want people to share knowledge, you need to reward them for sharing knowledge.

"Instead of just KPIs, consider also adding BPIs (behavior personal indicators). How do they behave in the team dynamic? Look at these BPIs when rewarding your people, when you're looking at who's accelerating and who's progressing. Encourage knowledge share and reward people for knowledge sharing."

—Arlette Bentzen, Chief Happiness Officer at Arbejdsglæde

Why Are Relationships So Important?

The emotional system of the brain evolved with the specific purpose of enabling us to cooperate in social groups. Its primary role is to create bonding between us. We constantly respond to our emotional environment. From our early years, our emotional systems are shaped by interaction with others. Parents and primary caregivers have a huge impact on the emotional template developed in our brains over the first three years of our lives.

Thereafter, this process continues as we constantly refine our emotional processing and responses to handle the changing world in which we live. In organizations, we have a deep-rooted need to experience fulfilling relationships with those with whom we spend the most time. This includes our colleagues, our line managers, and our teams.

How Can Organizations Respond?

It is vital to have direct, personal data understanding of how employees feel about these relationships. Both positive experiences and relationship challenges need to be understood and discussed in a safe, trusted environment. Many working relationships can be improved through mutual understanding, including communication styles and preferences.

Third-party facilitation can also be very helpful, provided it is handled in a supportive, nonjudgmental way. It is completely reasonable for misunderstandings to occur in our working lives. A culture of early constructive intervention is much more productive than formalized mediation when positions have already become entrenched.

Summary

Whatever an individual's personality, relationships are important to all human beings. Some of us enjoy the quiet and periods of isolation, but we will all eventually want to leave the cave to seek connection through relationships.

As I shared in my TEDx Talk in Brighton, we also learned from our data that we are the average happiness of those closest to us. That can be our family, friends, and colleagues. The next time you change jobs, seriously consider the happiness of the current employees. It could impact you in more ways than you know.

Companies can dismiss websites like Glassdoor as much as they like (and they are clearly not perfect), but sites like these do impact how your employer brand is perceived. The way I see it, Glassdoor is where unhappy employees go to vent. It is much better to offer an internal opportunity for employees to vent, rather than on Glassdoor.

Every parent out there knows this: "You are as happy as your unhappiest child." In a modern society where not everyone seeks to be a parent, these deep connections can come from work colleagues or the people you meet volunteering on the weekends. Their happiness will impact your happiness, and vice versa.

Now that we have discussed our emotional needs, we next discuss our ability to reflect as human beings. It annoys me when politicians get attacked for changing their minds. There are many good reasons for holding politicians accountable, but we shouldn't demonize someone's ability to take stock, reflect on their views, and form a new opinion.

The more we criticize politicians and business leaders for changing their minds, the more we force them into having simple black-and-white views that fit into the most absurd of human inventions known as the left and right political spectrums. Human beings can do better than just shouting at each other, by looking for opportunities to listen and learn from each other. The same applies at work.

We have looked at the top four drivers of employee happiness, so now it's time to review the top four drivers of employee engagement, starting with what we call the reflective system, commencing with purpose.

Notes

1. https://phys.org/news/2022-10-scientists-nobel-prize-physics-quantum.html?_escaped_fragment_=&deviceType=desktop
2. Denise M. Rousseau and Kimberly Ling, "Commentary: Following the resources in positive organizational relationships," in *Exploring Positive Relationships at Work* (Psychology Press, 2006), pp. 373–384.
3. Ruth Blatt and Carl T. Camden, "Positive relationships and cultivating community," in *Exploring Positive Relationships at Work* (Psychology Press, 2006), pp. 243–264.
4. Kathleen L. McGinn, "History, structure, and practices: San Pedro longshoremen in the face of change," in *Exploring Positive Relationships at Work* (Psychology Press, 2006), pp. 265–276.
5. Hannah Higgins and Douglas Kahn, *Mainframe Experimentalism: Early Computing and the Foundations of the Digital Arts* (University of California Press, 2012).

6. Belle Ragins and Amy Verbos, *Exploring Positive Relationships at Work: Building a Theoretical and Research Foundation,* Jane E. Dutton and Belle Rose Ragins, eds. (Psychology Press, 2017).

7. https://vimeo.com/752745137

8. Kerstin Alfes, Catherine Truss, Emma C. Rees Soane, and Mark Gatenby, "The relationship between line manager behavior, perceived HRM practices, and individual performance: Examining the mediating role of engagement," *Human Resource Management* 52 (no. 6): 839–859, https://doi.org/10.1002/hrm.21512

CHAPTER 9

Aligned Meaning and Purpose

Purpose has been a bit of a buzzword over the last few years (for good reason) and sometimes people mistakenly think it belongs on the happiness side of the employee engagement and happiness triangle. However, our purpose in life and work is associated with the direction system of our brain. It is partly why, when people feel they don't have a purpose, they describe it as being lost in life.

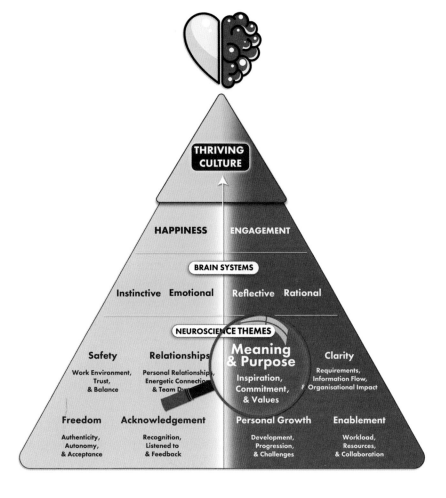

Purpose is key to direction and our brains need it to function in a high-performance way.

What Are Meaning and Purpose?

Meaning denotes something of personal value and importance, offering information or an experience that's relevant to making sense of our life journey. Purpose addresses the "why" question: it represents the perceived reason for doing something, offering the potential of a result that's personally relevant and sustaining. Meaning is more of an internal motivator, while purpose is something we can take into the world.

Meaning and purpose provide humans with a connection, it's why we attach ourselves to organizations and causes. This is evidenced by looking at the Meaning and Purpose scores by sector in The Happiness Index study. The Health and Wellbeing sector was by far the highest-scoring sector, with an average score of 8.9. This is because workers in this sector felt "inspired" by their work and were highly "committed" to helping their organization succeed.

Consider these specific insights from our study:

- **Customer Insight 1:** "Our customer team shared with us recently that one of the things they noticed across all the different industries we work with is that behaviors, values, and purpose are only really tested when an organization is going through tough times."

  I love this insight from the team, because it shows how important these factors are to organizational resilience.

- **Customer Insight 2:** "Sentiment regarding inspiration often scores toward the lower end in our dataset. We often see customers make changes to counteract this that has a big impact. An interesting thing happens when an organization shares its weaknesses. We often see organizations worry that low scores will spread negativity, but what is more likely to happen is the organization seems relatable and this can lead to higher inspirational scores."

▲ Question ▲	▼	Science & Technology ▲▼	Food & Drinks ▲▼	Public Service ▲▼	Commerce ▲▼	Health & Well-being
19 Meaning & Purpose		8.0	8.1	7.2	7.0	8.3	8.9
20 How inspired are you by your organization?		7.4	7.5	6.2	5.4	7.3	8.5
21 How committed are you to helping the organization succeed?		8.7	8.8	8.2	8.7	9.3	9.3

Within meaning and purpose, this chapter drills down into three subareas:

- Inspiration
- Commitment
- Values

INSPIRATION

Inspiration is the inner sensation that motivates us to do something important, a state where we are prepared to engage with a significant challenge regardless of the difficulties it may present. When we are inspired, we have the potential to be our best and to summon all of our personal talent. Inspiration can be triggered by our external experience or by our own internal thoughts.

From working with hundreds of CEOs and HR directors over the last 15 years, one of my observations is that employees don't want their leaders to be perfect. In fact, some of the most inspirational leaders I have worked with would probably not fit the mold of textbook leaders.

This might sound odd, but I was at a customer all-company meeting recently and it hit me how loved the CEO was and how loyal their employees were. I know people don't like to use the word "love" in a work context, but I could see it in their eyes and in their words. They loved their leader.

People in this particular organization had routinely worked there for 5 to 10 or more years. When I spoke to the team, they all acknowledged their leader had plenty of flaws but this is part of why they worked in this company.

Perhaps as human beings full of odd quirks ourselves, we like our leaders and organizations to reflect that?

External Research

If I have learned one thing over the last few crazy years, it is that inspiration must come from within. Although inspirational leaders certainly exist, ultimately that drive needs to be found inside each person. As organizations have become more distributed across the globe, the need for inspiration not to be reliant on a few charismatic individuals has increased.

It wasn't until I interviewed author and media commentator Carolyn Hobdey (the founder of MayDey Limited and COO of 15ten15) on followership that my mind was opened up to the importance of *followership*, which is the opposite of leadership. We have millions of books on leadership, but very few on followership.

Tom Nixon, in his book *Work with Source*, illustrates the importance of founders helping others find the source of their energy and being intentional about passing it on when there is a leadership change. Inspiration is not something that a leader must "do" to people, because all humans have the innate ability to connect to inspiration.

Source is about fostering a culture where this natural inspiration can ignite creativity. One of the most powerful things you can do to develop an inspired, energized workplace is to create the conditions, for those who want to, to express what their individual soul is telling them that the world most needs from them, and that they feel the most passion to do. Encourage them to use this as their personal North Star as they evolve their own contributions to the collective endeavour. It's not just an individual process.

Back in 1985, Bernard Bass found that:

> transformational leadership is important for follower work engagement and performance because it encourages agentic follower behavior such as strengths use and personal initiative. . . .This helps followers perform well because they are able to mobilize the energy and enthusiasm to remain focused. As proposed by the full-range leadership model, through transformational leadership, leaders truly seem to "transform" followers because followers are stimulated to use their character strengths and lead themselves.[1]

Expert View

"Inspiration comes from linking everything to the vision and being clear on your purpose. No matter your role or title, you should be aware of who the brand is, its purpose, why you're in the brand, and what value you bring. Be open and transparent about this on a regular basis to inspire others to tell their story. As soon as people start having these discussions, the dialogue about your *why*, and your purpose, both personally and professionally, create an environment where people feel they can be themselves."

—Rob Turner, Culture and Engagement Manager, BT

COMMITMENT

Commitment is the state of emotional attachment to a cause. It is something we feel as a sense of belonging and purpose, which is personally meaningful to our own life journey. It is a state of emotional engagement where we identify with a wider human group or purpose. At its higher energetic level, it can be described as passion.

External Research

In "Leadership Styles, Psychological Factors, and Employee Commitment to Service Quality in the Hotel Industry," Md Karim Rabiul and colleagues state:

> This study examines the mediating role of psychological meaningfulness and safety between leadership styles and commitment to service quality (ECSQ) drawing on self-concept theory.
>
> A total of 446 hotel employees working in the hotel industry in Bangladesh participated in a cross-sectional survey. The test reveals the differences between the servant and transactional leadership styles. Transactional leaders do not positively influence ECSQ directly, but do so through psychological meaningfulness, and not through psychological safety. The results of the study imply that hospitality professionals should concentrate on developing psychologically safe and meaningful work environments by inculcating the servant leadership style.[2]

Expert View

"Rejection leads to redirection. We are rejecting a world which focuses only on shareholder value and profiteering by the few. Redirection is leading to business models that attract and retain people who want a life alongside their work, not before it and a sustainable living. Smart business leaders are awake to this change and hiring the smart talent who want a better life, but more needs to happen. We live in a world of instant gratification; how about rejecting this for a world of eternal gratefulness? If I had a message for the world, it would be: 'Trust more, fear less. By being fearless, we commit.'"

—John Fitzgerald, MD Harmonics

VALUES

We develop our personal values through life, and especially in our younger years. They are our emotional guide that help us know what we want to experience in terms of human connection and concepts such as fairness. Sharing our sense of values is critical to sustaining team journeys where we are engaging with others who want to share the same emotional experiences as ourselves.

External Research

In the paper "Company Values in HRM," Pekka Pitkänen found:

Value programs are used in various strategic purposes, but they are rarely implemented in a way that gives full benefit for the company.

It was found that companies tend to focus on either core/cornerstone values, or internal/operational values, but rarely have both working together for full benefit.

Cornerstone values were used to ground the company and give its employees a clear direction for the long-term. Companies with cornerstone values saw increased employee satisfaction in the long term, as well as minor benefits in value driven decision making. Operational values, on the other hand, were used to guide the everyday behavior of the employees in a way that best supports the long-term vision and mission of the company.

Operational values greatly benefitted the company culture and climate, proving a strong tool for strategic human resource management.

It was also found that evaluation of the value program was very important, not only in continuous improvement, but also for the credibility of the entire program. Employees pay special attention to the evaluation of value programs, as a measure of their importance for the management, and thus the company.[3]

Expert View

"The pandemic awoke people to the fact, as Oliver Burkeman put it, that if we live to 80 we only have 4,000 weeks on this planet. Your employees have had time to contemplate this fact and it is why now more than ever helping your employees understand the purpose of your organization is key to helping them feel engaged and happy.

"Consider purpose as the North Star. Purpose is about direction and should lead and inform your decision-making. Purpose essentially describes who you want to be. Your values describe why your purpose is important to you; there needs to be cohesion between the North Star direction and your values. It is your job as a leader to elegantly elevate purpose, facilitate healthy debate, and connect the dots between people and ideas."

—Minter Dial, Author, Strategist, and Brand Expert

Why Are Meaning and Purpose So Important?

All three factors are essential to human motivation. When we are able to align our own sense of meaning with a purpose that can be activated in the external world, we are well positioned to give our best. The reflective system of the brain is the home of our sense of wholeness and self, where we can be imaginative and expansive in our thoughts. It is the world of our conscious aspirations, our hopes, and our dreams of self-fulfillment. Tapping into this potential can impact an organization's success. Typical areas to focus our attention on in this context are inspiration, commitment, and values.

How Can Organizations Respond?

The foundational requirement is to get to know employees for who they are, not just their job roles or titles. Ongoing dialogue to build a collective understanding of these motivators can be part of systematic processes, such as personal development sessions, but the depth of discovery needs to be much more meaningful and flexible than typically prescriptive performance appraisal systems. This extends well beyond semiformal routines to become a natural part of our daily work experiences, with those in leadership roles equipped with the desire, skills, and perspective to regard this as a normal part of their roles.

Summary

Purpose is linked to direction and can be hard to find. It is also worth remembering that it is not always obvious what an individual's purpose is.

I remember footballer Emmanuel Adebayor being constantly criticized for being a money grabber during his playing career. In fact, if you dug a little deeper and listened to him, he made it clear that he wanted to earn as much money as possible because he could use that money for charitable work related to his religious beliefs back home in Togo.

"Everything I do in life I put in the hands of God, my Creator. He gave me the chance to be where I am today and He's the one that can take it all away from me. There is nothing more important for me than God." Adebayor was driven by a purpose not found in his day-to-day role. Whatever your views on religion, it was clear he was driven by a purpose outside football.

The moral of the story is that money can serve a purpose, but don't leap to the conclusion that a person seeking the highest-paid job is motivated only by money.

Next up, personal growth.

Notes

1. https://www.sciencedirect.com/science/article/pii/S0263237322000603
2. Md Karim Rabiul, Ataul Karim Patwary et al., "Leadership styles, psychological factors, and employee commitment to service quality in the hotel industry," *Journal of Quality Assurance in Hospitality & Tourism* 23 (no. 4): 853–881, https://www.tandfonline.com/doi/full/10.1080/1528008X.2021.1913695
3. Pekka Pitkänen, "Company values in HRM: The use of company values in increase the effectiveness of human resource management," Aalto University, https://aaltodoc.aalto.fi/handle/123456789/32573

CHAPTER 10

Opportunities for Growth

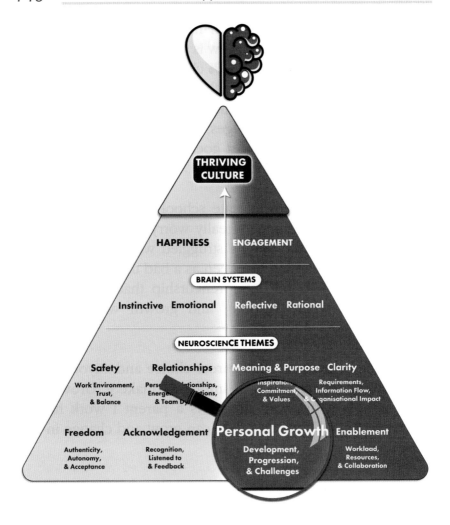

For organizations, understanding growth is key.

What Is Personal Growth?

In this context, we are referring to the process of fulfilling and expressing our wider potential. Opportunities for growth are therefore ones that offer us new experiences, challenges, and opportunities to learn.

As humans, we need to feel a sense of personal growth. However, in our survey, personal growth was the joint lowest-scoring theme (7.2), because topics such as "opportunities to progress" and "training opportunities" are polarizing.

The standard deviation for these topics is high, meaning that people have opposing views. Some organizations score well and some score poorly. By reviewing the comments, we saw a divide between people taking ownership of their own growth and others who felt it is the organization's responsibility to provide these opportunities.

Consider these specific insights from our study:

- **Customer Insight 1:** "Personal growth questions often score low in our dataset. One employee said that they felt the company treated personal growth as important but not a priority. They used this statement to show employees their personal growth was both important and a priority. This organization managed to turn a negative into a positive by harnessing the feedback and acting on it."
- **Customer Insight 2:** "One constant theme we see across our surveys is that personal growth scores tend to score toward the lower end. A key reason for this is people want to develop but they feel their current workload does not allow for this. Companies carving time out for personal growth often see their scores improve quickly."

Engagement			
How satisfied are you with the amount of learning opportunities on offer? (Reflective)	20339	7.2	2.4
How satisfied are you with the opportunity to progress your career here? (Reflective)	20340	6.8	2.6

Next time you go to a commercial growth meeting, ask tough questions about how much time is being made for personal and career progression. They work hand in hand.

> ### Expert View
>
> "When hiring, consider looking for smart people who meet about 60% of the job brief and then give them that extra 40% to grow into. No employee is ever the finished article, and looking for perfect human cyborgs who 100% fit our roles is doomed to fail. Broadening up your approach will help employees see an opportunity to progress and help you recruit a more diverse team."
>
> —Andrew MacAskill, CCO at Fraser Dove International

CHALLENGES

To maintain a sense of momentum, we need to feel appropriately challenged in our roles. The key is achieving the right balance. Feeling a little outside of our personal comfort zone is a good place for personal growth because we have to engage our wider potential to succeed. If this goes too far, we will retreat into survival mode, where we resist change and new demands.

External Research

The Happiness Index measures the entire employee life cycle, from onboarding to exit. One of the most common reasons we see people leave an organization is a situation where they don't feel their role challenges them. Striking a balance between challenging employees and pushing them too far is complex, and the data shows that organizations struggle in this area.

My advice is to ask people. Keep the dialogue open in relation to how your employees feel about their roles and whether they feel challenged in their work.

Expert View

"I learnt in my earlier career that always asking myself and others for permission can be a barrier to growth. It is important to have a growth mindset in order to see challenges as opportunities."

—Njabulo Mashigo, Executive HR Director, Vodacom (part of Vodaphone)

Why Are Growth Opportunities So Important?

We are built to grow and to explore the boundaries of our capabilities. This is a reflection of both our evolutionary instinct and our need for personal meaning. People need to see opportunities for exploration and discovery. If we stand still, we stagnate. By the same token, employees need to feel they are learning and developing. The work they do needs to stretch and energize them.

How Can Organizations Respond?

The traditionally recognized need for systematic processes around career development and succession planning remains. This is not just about promotion or formalized career progression, but also about instances in the current job situation where people can be asked to develop new talents to contribute to their role. Particularly significant is the need to offer a meaningful and ongoing learning experience. This is how we all stay alert and keep our instincts for learning primed.

Summary

Growth is one of the areas that we most commonly see organizations struggle with. Getting this area right can have huge benefits for your organization. Personal growth greatly increases your staff attraction and retention rates.

Remember to bake growth and learning opportunities into your employer brand. In the quantum chapter of my first book, *Freedom to Be Happy,* I called this embedded learning.

This chapter ends the reflective section. Now we move to rational systems. In the next chapter, we'll discuss clarity. It's not always the most fashionable factor, but it's one of the most important factors for organizational success.

Notes

1. Makoto Matsuo, "Influences of developmental job experience and learning goal orientation on employee creativity: Mediating role of psychological empowerment," *Human Resource Development International* 25 (no. 1): 4–18, https://doi.org/10.1080/13678868.2020.1824449

2. Domitille Bonneton, et al., "Do global talent management programs help to retain talent? A career-related framework." *International Journal of Human Resource Management* 33 (no. 2): 203–238, https://doi.org/10.1080/09585192.2019 .1683048

CHAPTER 11

Clarity

Imagine traveling to a gig to see your favorite band but not knowing what city the event was in. Now imagine not knowing what time it starts or how you're going to get there. That would be stressful, right? Well this type of thing happens in organizations all the time.

Of the top eight needs, clarity is the simplest to understand, but its importance is often underestimated in helping employees feel engaged at work.

Companies make assumptions, including assuming that employees know what is expected of them. It's obvious what your organization does and what your employees need to do, right? You give them job descriptions, after all.

This is a very common mistake that we see in the data and throughout organizations. I also know this because it is one area that I and other founders across the world routinely mess up on. The closer you are to running an organization, the easier it is to forget that not everyone is privy to the information that you are.

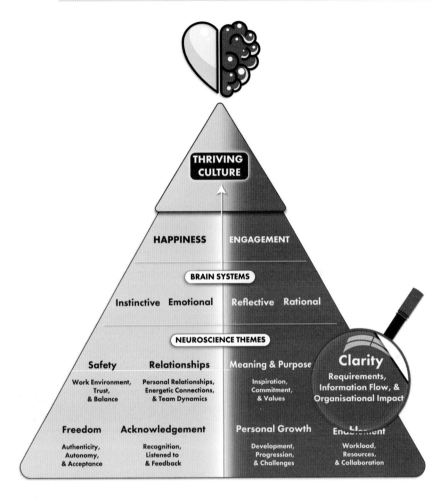

Never assume anything. Work hard to offer clarity from the recruitment process all the way through the performance review. Employees vary on how much detail they want, but conveying the big picture is important to driving employee engagement.

What Is Clarity?

Clarity is the ability to think without distraction and to concentrate on relevant information and tasks. Clarity is important for employees, and is one of our highest-scoring themes (8.0), meaning that the clarity needs of employees are regularly being met. Clarity helps them to understand what they need to do and when to do it.

There are three key areas to clarity, two of which score very well:

- Requirements of your job (8.5): This is where job descriptions and regular reviews come into play.
- Link between your role and the organization's success (8.0): This is a key motivator for people.

The area that often needs improving is "Being Kept Informed" (7.5), which builds trust and understanding among employees.

Consider these specific insights from our study:

- **Customer Insight 1:** "We typically see that areas that score low for feeling informed about what's happening in their company are often those that are furthest away from the message. This is normally those furthest from leadership (the source of the message).The more layers and different people this message goes through, the more it can become diluted and misinterpreted. Organizations that focus on internal comms start to improve this area."
- **Customer Insight 2:** Cakes and Clarity: "We know perks alone will not drive a culture forward. Perks, like the presentation of a Victoria sponge, are nice, but it is the taste and structural integrity of the fruity gateau, the cultural pillars, that give it its strength and long-lasting impact. But if those 'perks' are sprinkled, with care, onto foundational layers of psychological safety, clarity, and enablement, to name a few, like any good cultural bakeoff, they will be the icing on the cake."

Highs & Lows: Factors

Each question in the Cultural Assessment is linked to a factor. Below you'll see your results split into your strongest factors and those where you can make improvements.

Highest-Scoring Factors	Av. Rating	Lowest-Scoring Factors	Av. Rating
Committed to helping organizations (Meaning & Purpose)	8.8	Opportunities to progress (Personal Growth)	6.8
Getting on with people (Relationships)	8.6	Opinions listened to (Acknowledgment)	7.1
Enjoyment (Relationships)	8.5	Training (Personal Growth)	7.2
Requirements of your job (Clarity)	8.5	Work and home-life balance (Safety)	7.2
Positive relationships (Relationships)	8.3	Valued as an individual (Acknowledgment)	7.2
Link between your role and organizational success (Clarity)	8.0	Inspiration (Meaning & Purpose)	7.2
Your true self at work (Freedom)	7.9	Kept informed (Clarity)	7.5
Manage workload (Enablement)	7.9	Access to the resources you need (Enablement)	7.6
Freedom in role (Freedom)	7.8	Trust (Safety)	7.7
Challenge in role (Personal Growth)	7.7	Physical environment (Safety)	7.7

Within clarity, this chapter drills down into three subareas:

- Job requirements
- Information flow
- Organizational impact

JOB REQUIREMENTS

Each person needs to understand exactly what is expected of them in their role, an area classically explained in the job description, including key tasks and responsibilities. Importantly, such documents should be dynamic and evolve over time, keeping pace with the person's learning and ability to contribute.

External Research

In 2001, Low and colleagues found that role clarity is a key predictor of employee behavior: "Ambiguous demands or unclear expectations are related to low commitment to the organization's goals and values."[1]

In 2015, Lee and Nasurdin stated: "Conversely, role clarity has a positive relationship to an individual's motivation to apply effort toward task performance."[2]

Let's take the role of the salesperson. It might seem obvious what a salesperson does: sell. Apply that to other roles. What does a nurse do? Is their job to nurse? Not as easy as you first thought to define such roles. What about an engineer? Is their role to engineer? Engineer what? There is a big difference between the expectations of a software engineer and a railway engineer, for example.

For some reason, role clarity for salespeople is not taken seriously as in other roles. I put some of this down to work role snobbery, which is odd considering most of our roles depend on someone selling something to someone else down the road.

As we delved into the research, it became clearer and clearer that role clarity is important for every single role.

Expert View

"Always start with a clear job description that everyone agrees on. A clear understanding of an employee's role and responsibilities is the starting point on the path to engaged employees. You will be surprised how many organizations forget to start here."

—Gemma Shambler, Head of People at The Happiness Index

INFORMATION FLOW

People need to have access to the right information to enable them to do their jobs effectively. This needs to include primary information for task execution and supporting information to provide context. The contextual information offers room for more creative ideas as to how task responsibilities can evolve.

Happiness Index recorded a benchmark of 7.7 for happiness, HR professionals rated their overall happiness at work at 6.8 on average.

When we dug deeper, we found that the happiness of HR professionals falls if they don't feel their work is having a positive impact.

Expert View

"As an employee, understanding where your work fits in and delivers impact against the wider goal of the organization is key for employees to feel engaged in their work. Organizations are in constant flux, so it is important to continually check in and offer clarity on how your team members are contributing to the bigger picture. Feeling connected to the bigger goal can help us all feel a sense of pride in our work and achievement in reaching our goals."

—Fiona McDonnell, International General Manager, Board Advisor, Author, VP at Booking.com

Why Is Clarity So Important?

Human capacity for rational thought is far more advanced than any other living species and this is reflected in the size and sophistication of the human cortex. Rational thought is concerned with interpretation and execution, ultimately with getting things done. Its role is essentially practical. We have the capacity for action at a more basic instinctive level, but this is where we establish the rules of execution for the complex capabilities we learn through life. Once task skills are mastered, much of this processing takes place at a subconscious level, such as using a keyboard or driving a car.

How Can Organizations Respond?

We need to be clear about all the relevant factors in order to take appropriate and effective action. The neural pathways we create in our brains are our rules of engagement. To perform at our best we need clarity on matters like what is expected of us, what outcomes we are looking for, what authority we have, who we are expected to engage with, what information we have access to, and so on. Examining how organizations handle the communication of people requirements, information flow, and organizational impact is critical in this context.

Summary

Without clarity, your team can feel stressed and confused. Worse than that, they could be working hard in the wrong direction.

Imagine you are flying from London to New York for a gig, but you find out the gig is actually in Hong Kong. Clarity is key, so you don't end up wasting energy or working hard in the wrong direction.

In the next chapter, we finish the rational section by covering enablement.

Notes

1. Chongho Lee, Myungsook An, and Yonghwi Noh, "The effects of emotional display rules on flight attendants' emotional labor strategy, job burnout and performance," *Service Business* 9 (no. 3), https//doi.org/10.1007/s11628-014-0231-4

2. Aizzat Nasurdin, Noor Ahmad, Cheng Tan, "Cultivating service-oriented citizenship behavior among hotel employees: The instrumental roles of training and compensation, *Service Business* 9 (no. 2), 343–360, DOI: 10.1007/s11628-014-0230-5

3. Ron Westrum, "The study of information flow: A personal journey," *Safety Science* 67 (August 2014): 58–63, https://doi.org/10.1016/j.ssci.2014.01.009

4. Šujanová et al., cited in Nidhi Gupta, Kapil Pandla, and J. P. Nautiyal, "Role of communication in enhancing workplace happiness: A review of literature," *International Journal of Research Publication and Reviews* 3 (no. 1): 1366–1370, https://ijrpr.com/uploads/V3ISSUE1/IJRPR2504.pdf

5. Nidhi Gupta, Kapil Pandla, and J. P. Nautiyal, "Role of communication in enhancing workplace happiness: a review of literature," *International Journal of Research Publication and Reviews* 3 (no. 1): 1366–1370, https://ijrpr.com/uploads/V3ISSUE1/IJRPR2504.pdf

CHAPTER 12

Enablement to Succeed

Enablement is the last of the eight themes and completes the rational needs section.

So, now you know that your gig is in Tokyo and it starts at 8:00 p.m. The question is, do you have the tools to get there? Do you have a budget for the ticket? Are there any available seats on the flight?

Pointing the team in the right direction is just the beginning. You also need to give them the tools to do their job. You can't send someone on a mission to the North Pole wearing flip-flops, can you?

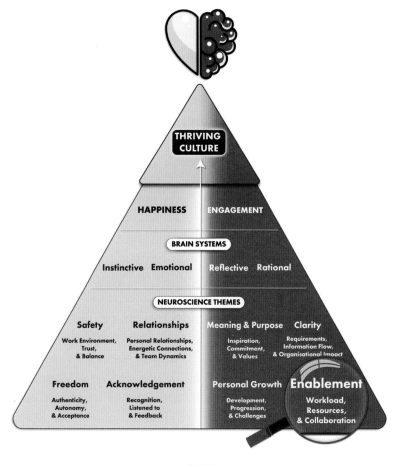

Getting the right resources to your teams at the right time is key for employee engagement; it's ultimately the precursor to whether an organization succeeds or fails.

What Is Enablement?

Enablement means having the necessary resources to get the job done.

Enablement is all about putting employees in the best possible position to succeed. The Happiness Index study looked at whether employees are able to "Manage their workload" and whether they have "Access to the resources they need." Across our data universe, enablement is a mid-ranking theme, with a score of 7.7.

However, when we look at it from the sector level, the public service sector scores are considerably lower than others. Employees in this sector feel they are unable to manage their workload and are under-resourced, which is not allowing them to succeed in their role.

Consider these specific insights from our study:

- **Customer Insight 1:** Commitment versus resources: "We often see an association between commitment and resources. If companies fail to supply the correct resources for employees to do their job, we see that commitment levels drop quickly. Don't expect employees to be committed if you have not given them the tools to do the job."
- **Customer Insight 2:** "We often see in customer data that when an employee's workload is too high, energy levels drop. When energy levels drop, we see this negatively impacts relationships. Obvious really but

worth considering the hidden cost of not hiring or hiring too late as workload increases."

▲ Question ▲▼	▲▼	Science & Technology ▲▼	Food & Drinks ▲▼	Public Service
19 Clarity	7.9	8.0	7.6	7.0
20 How clear are you on the requirements of your job?	8.2	8.3	8.4	7.9
21 How well does your organization keep you informed?	7.6	7.3	6.9	6.3
23 Enablement	7.5	7.6	7.4	65
24 How able are you to manage your workload?	7.6	7.7	7.6	6.7
24 To what extent do you have access to the resources you need to support you in your role?	7.4	7.5	7.2	6.5

Within enablement, this chapter drills down into three subareas:

- Workload
- Resources
- Collaboration

WORKLOAD

An employee's workload and the degree of challenge needs to be sufficient to keep the person engaged but not overwhelmed. People need to be in a position where they have a realistic chance of handling their workload successfully and feeling a sense of achievement. Factors such as effective scheduling, task allocation, and prioritization are critical.

External Research

In "Lived Experiences of Mental Workload in Everyday Life," Serena Midha and the team at the University of Nottingham explained:

> Findings suggest that considering mental workload from a holistic and person-orientated perspective is important for understanding aspects of our wellbeing and task performances. Based on a mental workload cycle, healthy and efficient outcomes come from aiming to fluctuate between MWL levels in particular patterns, as this prevents the negative implications resulting from sustaining any level for too long whilst enabling the positive implications that each level can provide.[1]

Personally this is something I have had to get better at myself and I have slowly improved in this area over time. For example, I have been writing this book alongside my role as co-CEO of The Happiness Index. If I was to continue writing full time alongside my day-to-day role, it would not be sustainable for either of the roles and would interfere with my mental health. The process of writing this book has been enjoyable for short periods of time but has taken up a lot of my evenings and weekends that are important for my family and my mental health.

Considering your own workload and that of your team is crucial. Trying to sprint a marathon is not a good idea.

Expert View

"The key areas to get right for workload are agreeing on your focus and therefore your prioritization. It is also important to remember that we are not born to be good at scheduling our time, allocating tasks, and prioritizing our work. All of these skills can be learned, and it is important to support employees to improve in this area.

> "Technology has created a world that demands our instant attention and we need to learn skills to help us focus on the activities that will help us achieve our long-term goals."
>
> —Azzy Aslam, Performance Habits Coach at Comentra

RESOURCES

People need the right resources to be available to fulfil their responsibilities. This includes having access to the appropriate tools, systems, and support services, as well as enablement through education and training.

External Research

In "The Impact of Management Methods on Employee Engagement," Małgorzata Baran and Barbara Sypniewska found:

> Work engagement by Schaufeli is embedded in Hobfoll's theory of resources. There is a positive relationship between resources and commitment regarding aspects such as: help in achieving goals, reduction of requirements and control, support from superiors. Demerouti found that job resources such as performance feedback, supervisor support were predictors of engagement.
>
> Managers need to provide employees with resources and benefits that will oblige them to reciprocate in kind with higher levels of engagement. Although the results of this study highlight the importance of job characteristics and social support, there might be other factors that are more important for different employees. Thus, a "one size fits all" approach to employee engagement might not be the most effective. Managers should find out what resources and benefits are most desired by employees and most likely to create a sense of obligation that is returned with greater levels of engagement.[2]

Expert View

"Organizations need to learn how to become CROs (chief repetition officers) and tell the story of why the change has come about and how it impacts people, which will help socialization and bring people on board. Even now, many companies still do change management badly and pay the consequences. Some elements that are necessary for successful change:

- ◆ Time and opportunity for employees to reflect on their current mindset and how it might need to change
- ◆ Space for employees to discuss the shift and share their thoughts and experiences with each other"

—Sope Agbelusi, Executive Coach at MindsetShift

COLLABORATION

Collaboration with other teams outside of the immediate job role context can open up opportunities for wider creative contribution and more effective teamwork across the organization. Apart from new ideas that can emerge for greater efficiency and business success, this can also provide real cultural benefits and broader organizational agility.

External Research

Research out of Dhofar University in Oman[3] listed these supporting skills for successful teams to collaborate effectively:

- • Trust among all team members
- • Well-prepared to engage in various debates around ideas
- • Learning to commit to decisions and plans of action

- Effective leadership and structure of teams with well-defined roles and responsibilities of team members
- Proper performance evaluation of team members and rewards and recognition for outstanding work
- Focusing on achieving collective results

Expert View

"Collaboration is actually the thing that separates us from the beasts. In reality, it's what makes humankind so human, Good collaboration leads to innovation, which then itself leads to engagement and happiness."

—Dan Sodergren, Your Flock

Why Is Enablement So Important?

While clarity focuses on the "what," enablement focuses on the "how." This means having access to the means to do your job well. This includes tools, training, techniques, processes, information, time, support, and guidance. It also includes opportunities to collaborate with appropriate colleagues and having reasonable workload patterns.

How Can Organizations Respond?

Employees are in the best position to see how working processes are operating. Are they efficient, logical, prioritized, and clearly understood? Tapping into this feedback can be very effective at the team and organizational level and much more effective than allowing frustration to build and a blame culture to develop. It can encourage a sense of ownership when employees are able to constructively present performance barriers and are given the opportunity to solve the problem, which is much better than abdicating the problem to someone else. Are there suitable response mechanisms in place to review feedback on these matters, such as team or process reviews and opportunities for on-the-job learning?

Summary

Enablement is giving your team what they need to get the job done. There is a really interesting observation in Mike Stroud's book *Survival of the Fittest*. Mike was the doctor who partnered Sir Ranulph Fiennes for their joint polar expedition.

One of Mike's responsibilities was to calculate how much kit they could take and balance that against how many calories of food they needed. The entire expedition was a calculation in enablement. For every bit of kit they packed, they had to weigh it physically and metaphorically against the extra calorie burn and additional load added to their sleds.

There is one amazing point in the book where they calculate that a human dragging a sled can generate enough internal heat to keep themselves warm while outside their tents. This data calculation meant they decided not to pack their big winter coats and therefore save on weight. Think about that cold day when you go for a run or play a sport where you eventually need to remove a couple of the layers you added as your body warms up. A polar expedition is planned meticulously with all these micro-calculations in enablement considered. However, this calculation goes horribly wrong when the expedition grinds to a halt and they are standing in the cold without a proper coat. The answer was to hurriedly erect their tents but it meant that once again their progress was stopped.

For me this makes the point that data must meet experience at some point. All the data said not to pack the big coats, but if they had consulted my mum, they would have been wisely advised to "put your coat on," as she told me continually for a dozen years. Funnily enough, I spent five minutes this morning saying to my daughter Izzy, "Put your coat on."

Enablement is a trade-off between speed, time, and available budget, so remember to consult the data, talk to your team, and share your experiences. Failing all of that, give Patricia Phelan a call and ask her advice. She's always right.

Enablement completes our eight happiness and engagement themes.

The next chapters discuss how you blend this together throughout your organization to create the right conditions for a thriving culture to take root and flourish, whatever the environment.

Notes

1. Serena Midha, Max L. Wilson, and Sarah Sharples, "Lived experiences of mental workload in everyday life," *Proceedings of the 2022 CHI Conference on Human Factors in Computing Systems*, April 2022, https://dl.acm.org/doi/fullHtml/10.1145/3491102.3517690

2. Małgorzata Baran and Barbara Sypniewska, "The impact of management methods on employee engagement," *Sustainability* 12 (no. 1): 426, https://doi/.org/10.3390/su12010426

3. Awad Alhassan, Simona Floare Bora, and Yousif Abdelbagi Abdalla, "Collaboration with EAP teachers in English-medium instruction contexts in higher education: Content lecturer perspectives," *TESOL Journal* 13 (no. 1): e610, https://doi/.org/10.1002/tesj.610

Everything we have discussed thus far has been related to the universal needs of employees. We call these the universal needs of employee engagement and happiness and they are related to the human condition. This chapter discusses some of the most serious symptoms and challenges we see organizations face when these needs are not met.

These needs surface as organizational challenges in many different forms. Humanity and culture is constantly shifting and changing. Recall that happiness is a social factor, so solving serious issues like mental health and dismantling systemic racism are things we need to do together.

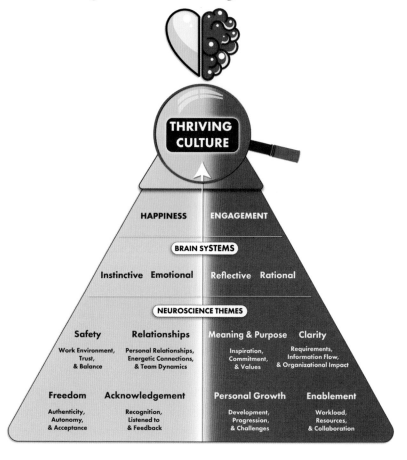

As social beings, what impacts those around us impacts all of us. You can choose to ignore them, but eventually they will impact you. When a colleague faces racism or sexual harassment, that is a problem not just for that individual but for all of us.

What Do Employees Care About?

This book covers the 8 key areas of employee engagement and happiness and the corresponding 24 subthemes. Now we discuss how these areas manifest themselves in the day-to-day conversations that organizations have the world over.

As mentioned in Chapter 1, recall that:

- Every organization in the world has unhappy employees.
- Every single human being has happiness levels that fluctuate up and down.
- No company will ever have happy employees all the time.
- It is not healthy for human beings to be happy all the time.
- Every organization in the world will be impacted by the topics in this book, whether or not they are aware of it.

Each section in this chapter is worthy of an entire book itself, but it is still important to touch on these subjects in order to frame the world we work in today. Let's look at some of the areas for which organizations are currently collecting data via The Happiness Index.

EMPLOYEE VOICE

The world has changed. Whether we like it or not, the 24/7 news culture is here and it directly impacts your employees. Employees want a voice to discuss the events that are important to them.

Here are a few stats that showcase the importance of listening to your employees:

- Motivation levels are 4.6 times higher in employees who feel listened to, according to *Inc.*[1]
- "The vast majority (86%) of employees feel people at their organization are not heard fairly or equally—and nearly half (47%) say that underrepresented voices remain undervalued by employers. In particular, essential workers, younger workers, non-caregiving employees, and employees who identify with underserved races and ethnicities feel less heard than their workplace counterparts."[2]
- Two in three (63%) employees feel their voice has been ignored in some way by their manager or employer, which may have a devastating impact on retention: A third (34%) of employees would rather quit or switch teams than voice their true concerns with management.[3]

If you want a motivated and engaged workforce, the first thing you need to do is to start listening to people. Once you give your employees a voice, you will have information and intelligence about what is important to them and you can better focus your efforts.

VISION AND VALUES

Organizations without clearly defined values are like ships without compasses—they are lost, with no sense of direction. Employees will struggle to help you achieve your vision and mission if they don't understand your values. This is detrimental to productivity and retention. Gather data on your values, understand any knowledge gaps, and formulate communication plans.

By getting a clear picture of where your organization stands with its vision and values, you can help your people convey this to your customers, thus ensuring repeat business and advocacy.

If you are currently focused on recruiting and attracting talent, it is important to understand that more than half the candidates out there will want to understand the vision and values of your organization. Underestimate the importance of outlining your vision and values at your peril. In fact, as reported by CNBC, 56% of employees won't consider a workplace that doesn't share their values.[4]

It is really important to sense-check your internal comms. It's not enough to have a vision and mission statement painted on the wall and just left for employees to read. Employees need to feel the values of the organization.

If your team does not understand where your organization is headed, you have an internal comms problem. This can lead to unengaged and unhappy employees, and ultimately lower productivity and customer service.

Employees and prospective employees want to understand your vision and values.

EQUALITY OF VOICE

In the UK, citizens are protected under the Equality Act 2010 from various types of discrimination. It is against the law to discriminate against someone because of:

- Age
- Disability
- Gender reassignment
- Marriage and civil partnership
- Pregnancy and maternity

- Race
- Religion or belief
- Sex
- Sexual orientation

In the United States, laws enforced by the Equal Employment Opportunity Commission (EEOC) protect similar groups and characteristics.

Understanding how your employees feel anonymously about these protected characteristics gives people a safe place to discuss any concerns they may have about their employee experience. It also allows companies to fix any problems before they become serious issues.

Think about employee concerns as if they're a small fire. Get to it early and a small cup of cold water can solve the problem. Get to them too late and you might need an entire fire brigade to help. Ignore fires completely and they could burn down your entire organization.

Here are some interesting stats for you:

- According to Glassdoor, 67% of job seekers consider workplace diversity an important factor when considering employment opportunities.[5]
- There are 26% higher profits in organizations with higher ethnic and cultural diversity, as cited in a study by McKinsey & Company.[6]

Discrimination
I don't know why, but it sometimes surprises people that employee happiness is closely linked to experiences with discrimination.

The first person to show me data on this was Professor Jeremy Dawson from Sheffield University in our interview based on his research at the NHS (National Health Service). Listen to the "Happiness and Humans" podcast episode called "Employee Happiness, infection rates, and patient mortality within the NHS" to learn more.

Although the NHS datasets are the largest in the world, the findings are pretty obvious when you think about. If you are discriminated against, it will make you unhappy. Happiness leads to performance, so it is clear that discrimination is both a moral and a performance issue.

Racial Equity and Racism

In the UK, the Commission on Race and Ethnic Disparities report landed in March 2021, declaring: "The country (UK) has come a long way in 50 years and the success of much of the ethnic minority population in education and, to a lesser extent, the economy, should be regarded as a model for other white-majority countries."[7]

This report started conversations between The Happiness Index and Sope Agbelusi (Mindset shift), Kevin Withane (DiveristyX), and Shereen Daniels (HR Rewired), who all shared that the report did not reflect their lived experiences.

We started to look at these problems and discuss the data that gave a real sense of the lived experience of employees. We wanted to understand how people really felt about racial equity.

Together with HR Rewired, we produced the Advancing Racial Equity report, which is a sobering document on how concerned employees are about this area. The full report can be downloaded from The Happiness Index website, Resources tab (or visit https://thehappinessindex.com/books/short-reads/racial-equity-report/).

This image shows how employee happiness varies based on ethnic group in a small sample of 566 people. More data is needed in this area, but the initial data collected is incredibly concerning.

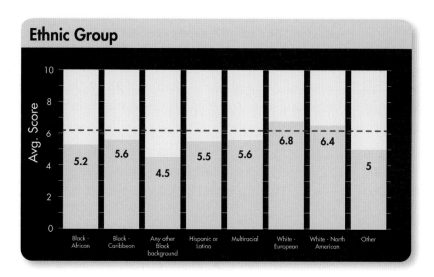

If you are looking for a starting point to understand racial equity and this data, I highly recommend picking up Shereen Daniel's book titled *The Anti-Racist Organization: Dismantling Systemic Racism in the Workplace*. My biggest lesson from Shereen is that we need to treat racism like a form of cancer. As Shereen explains in her book:

> There were no debates about whether they should treat my cancer. No other consultant barged into Dr. Shafi's office and demanded that he turn his attention to someone else.
>
> No other nurse complained that my tests were causing a backlog for other patients who had more serious symptoms than I had. The receptionist didn't argue that being specific about my cancer was being divisive. The cardiologist didn't chime in with "What about my patients?"
>
> There was no expectation for me to educate anyone on Hodgkin's lymphoma. And Dr. Shafi didn't gingerly tiptoe around naming my cancer.

He was very open about the mortality rates, possible complications, and such. Honesty. Transparency. No debates about whether they should "only" focus on my cancer. My cancer needed a specific intervention, a roster of individuals who offered more than empathy and a commitment to make a difference.
    —Racism, like cancer, needs specific intervention.[8]

Privilege

As a male with white privilege, I often find myself sending others who want to learn more about white privilege to this statement from John Amaechi, a psychologist, a *New York Times* best-selling author, and a former NBA basketball player: "There is nothing but a benefit to understanding our own privileges, white and otherwise. Having white privilege doesn't make your life easy, but understanding it can make you realize why some people's lives are harder than they should be."

I found this quote a really great starting point on my own journey to understanding more about white privilege. Like everyone in the history of the world, I have had struggles in my life, but I have never struggled due to the color of my skin. John also goes on to explain that there is no downside to understanding our privileges and I agree with that.

I still have a lot more to learn, and I think it is important that we all continue to educate ourselves on this subject.

EMPLOYEE WELL-BEING AND MENTAL HEALTH

When your people are stressed, exhausted, or feel disconnected from the workplace, it's detrimental to their health and happiness and, in turn, to your business performance.

- There is a 420% average ROI on mental health support in the workplace, per the UK government.
- According to Mind, a mental health organization in the UK, 21% of employees reported calling in sick due to workplace stress.[9]

- The London School of Economics and Political Science found that the annual cost of mental health problems to the UK economy was £118 billion.[10]

What's important is breaking the taboo. One of the most insidious things about mental health is that it often goes undiscussed. This is particularly true in the workplace, where emotions are seen as out of place. By asking your people about their mental health and how you can support their mental well-being, you're helping to dismantle this harmful paradigm.

THE "WHERE WE WORK" GAP

There is a huge gap between what senior executives think is right for their people and what employees need and want. Consider these statistics, for example:

- According to YouGov, 57% of employees want to be able to work from home.[11]
- The Office for National Statistics found that 47% of employees reported improved well-being as a result of increased home working.[12]
- According to Microsoft, "The source of this tension is clear as business leaders seek a return to what once was; 50% of leaders say their company already requires, or plans to require, full-time in-person work in the year ahead. This percentage is even higher for leaders in the manufacturing (55%), retail (54%), and consumer goods (53%) industries. This stands in sharp contrast to the data on the importance of flexible work to employees. Over half of respondents (52%) say they are likely to consider shifting to hybrid or remote work in the year ahead."[13]

I am writing this page from a community tea room that overlooks Myddelton House Gardens in North London with a gorgeous botanical garden that is open to the public. As I look out of the window, I can see the volunteer gardeners tending to the beds.

Tellingly, the gardeners are not instructing the plants what soil and how much sunlight they need. Think about your employees like a gardener thinks about their plants.

EMPLOYEE LIFECYCLE MANAGEMENT

Onboarding, exit, and employee retention are all extremely important points to collect data and listen. How employees think and feel about their experiences of working in your organization changes and evolves over time.

Consider these tidbits:

- There is an 82% increase in retention rates for organizations with great employee onboarding, according to Brandon Hall Group.[14]
- There is a 91% improvement in relationship by soliciting feedback from new hires, per Candidate Experience.[15]
- According to the Chartered Institute of Personnel and Development, there is a 15% average employee turnover per year dependent on industry.[16]
- According to People Management, "The majority (83 per cent) of chief HR officers say they face a significant talent retention problem, research by XpertHR in partnership with Executive Networks has found."[17]
- Only 4.4% of organizations use questionnaires to understand their departing employees, as an article in *Harvard Business Review* explained.[18]

Environmental, Social, and Governance (ESG) from the Employee Perspective

More and more of these factors have led to organizations asking The Happiness Index to report how their employees are feeling via The Happiness Index ESG report. Following is a quick summary of how employees look at these areas in The Happiness Index.

ENVIRONMENTAL SAFEGUARDS

How an organization safeguards the environment is becoming increasingly important to employees and customers, who want to understand the ESG standards of the companies they procure from and work for.

- **Environmental sustainability:** In the ESG assessment, organizations are assessed based on their impact on climate change and the organization's environment management systems.
- **Waste:** Organizations are evaluated on the amount of waste they create (paper, water, etc.) and their efforts to recycle.
- **Energy efficiency:** Assessments are made about the organizations' energy consumption and use of green tech and renewable energy sources, as well as their plans for reducing carbon emissions and the carbon intensity of their products and services.

SOCIAL IMPLICATIONS AND THE ORGANIZATION

This addresses how an organization treats its employees (including health and safety concerns), suppliers, and the communities around it.

- **Health and safety:** Organizations are evaluated on their management of workplace safety.
- **Labor diversity:** Organizations are assessed on their ability to attract and develop a skilled and diverse workforce.
- **Sourcing/supply chain human rights:** In this theme, organizations are assessed on the management and transparency of their supply chain (e.g. anti-bribery and corruption and modern-day slavery policies).
- **Employee personal data protection:** Assessments are made on the volume of personal data being held, how it's held, whether there are any vulnerabilities, and the potential for a data breach.

- **Community:** Organizations are assessed on their relationships with their local community and whether they give back.
- **Pay and benefits:** This section is not solely about salaries and bonuses; organizations are also assessed on other benefits such as access to health care.

GOVERNANCE

This addresses how an organization handles issues such as leadership, internal controls, and transparency of communications.

- **Trust in leadership:** Organizations are evaluated on the ethics of their leadership team.
- **Transparency of communications:** Organizations are assessed on transparency of their actions and communications.
- **Leadership governance:** Organizations are assessed on the oversight measures in place to ensure the leadership team is delivering the organization's strategy.
- **Transparency in the financial health of the organization:** Assessments are made on the transparency of the organization in relation to its revenue generation and costs.

WHAT ORGANIZATIONS CAN DO ABOUT ESG

Consider these ESG-related stats:

- According to NAVEX Global, only 50% of employees believe that their company performs effectively against environmental metrics.[19]
- According to PwC, 76% will stop buying from companies that treat the environment, employees, or their community poorly.[20]
- According to Bright Network, 81% of students consider businesses' commitment to reducing their impact on the environment when applying for jobs.[21]

Investors, employees, and customers alike are focusing on ESG more than ever. If your people don't understand what you're doing, or aren't buying into its effectiveness, you'll be losing out on all of the benefits it can bring.

Understanding what your team wants and needs from your ESG offering is critical. ESG is a huge area, so concentrating on the areas that are important to your employees helps focus efforts.

We are all energetically connected. Even if the factors in this chapter have not directly impacted you, they have and will impact you indirectly. Whether you like it or not, your colleagues' problems are your problems and you need to take them seriously. If you are serious about improving the work culture of your organization, it is only possible to do this as a team.

The list of issues in this section is long. However, if you think like Shereen and treat all areas like a specific type of cancer and have specific approaches to dealing with them, you give your company a chance of success.

The message is clear that employees care about the culture of the organization they work for. Employees don't expect your organization to be perfect, but they do expect you to listen and engage in areas that are important to them.

Summary
I don't think any of the subjects in this chapter will be fixed anytime soon, but we can work together to improve them day by day. I do know that organizations that ignore the subjects in this chapter will find it increasingly difficult to hire and keep happy and engaged employees.

Create safe spaces to listen to your employees to make them feel heard so they feel part of the future. A thriving culture takes time and effort.

In my first business, we assumed we had a strong culture, which meant we focused on other areas of the business. I learned the hard way that culture should always be your priority. Culture is everyone's responsibility, but it should be the number-one job of the CEO. Otherwise, all other areas—from operation to brand—will struggle to thrive. Don't make my mistake and take a thriving culture for granted.

If this chapter of employee concerns feels daunting, remember to start by listening to your employees. Then focus on making your employees feel safe.

Notes

1. Melanie Curtin, "Employees who feel heard are 4.6x more likely to feel empowered to do their best work," *Inc.,* https://www.inc.com/melanie-curtin/employees-who-feel-heard-are-46x-more-likely-to-feel-empowered-to-do-their-best-work.html
2. Workforce Institute, "New research: The heard and the heard-nots," https://workforceinstitute.org/new-research-the-heard-and-the-heard-nots/
3. Ibid.
4. Stephanie Dhue and Sharon Epperson, "Most workers want their employer to share their values—56% won't even consider a workplace that doesn't, survey finds," https://www.cnbc.com/2022/07/01/most-workers-want-their-employer-to-share-their-values.html
5. Glassdoor Team, "What job seekers really think about your diversity and inclusion stats, https://www.glassdoor.com/employers/blog/diversity/

6. Dame Vivian Hunt, Lareina Yee, Sara Prince, and Sundiatu Dixon-Fyle, "Delivering through diversity," https://www.mckinsey.com/capabilities/people-and-organizational-performance/our-insights/delivering-through-diversity

7. "Commission on Race and Ethnic Disparities: The report," https://assets.publishing.service.gov.uk/government/uploads/system/uploads/attachment_data/file/974507/20210331_-_CRED_Report_-_FINAL_-_Web_Accessible.pdf

8. Shereen Daniel, *The Anti-Racist Organization: Dismantling Systemic Racism in the Workplace* (John Wiley & Sons, 2022).

9. "Taking care of your staff," https://www.mind.org.uk/workplace/mental-health-at-work/taking-care-of-your-staff/

10. "Mental health problems cost UK economy at least £118 billion a year," https://www.lse.ac.uk/News/Latest-news-from-LSE/2022/c-Mar-22/Mental-health-problems-cost-UK-economy-at-least-118-billion-a-year-new-research

11. "One in five want to work from home full time after the pandemic," https://www.marketscreener.com/quote/stock/YOUGOV-PLC-4006933/news/YouGov-One-in-five-want-to-work-from-home-full-time-after-the-pandemic-32952571/

12. "Is hybrid working here to stay?" https://www.ons.gov.uk/employmentandlabourmarket/peopleinwork/employmentandemployeetypes/articles/ishybridworkingheretostay/2022-05-23

13. Microsoft 2022 Work Trend Index: Annual report, https://news.microsoft.com/wp-content/uploads/prod/sites/631/2022/03/WTI_AnnualReport_Extended_.pdf

14. Madeline Laurano, "The true cost of a bad hire," https://b2b-assets.glassdoor.com/the-true-cost-of-a-bad-hire.pdf

15. "10 employee onboarding statistics you must know in 2022," https://www.kallidus.com/resources/blog/10-employee-onboarding-statistics-you-must-know-in-2022/

16. "Employee turnover and retention," https://www.cipd
.co.uk/knowledge/strategy/resourcing/turnover-retention-
factsheet

17. Arunth Sriganthan, "Majority of HR professionals claim
retaining talent is a significant problem, research reveals,"
February 1, 2023, https://www.peoplemanagement.co
.uk/article/1811990/majority-hr-professionals-claim-
retaining-talent-significant-problem-research-reveals

18. Everett Spain, and Boris Groysberg, "Making exit interviews
count," https://hbr.org/2016/04/making-exit-interviews-count

19. NAVEX Inc., "Global survey finds businesses increasing
ESG commitments, spending," https://www.navex.com/
blog/article/environmental-social-governance-esg-
global-survey-findings/

20. PricewaterhouseCoopers, "Beyond compliance: Consumers
and employees want business to do more on ESG," https://
www.pwc.com/us/en/services/consulting/library/
consumer-intelligence-series/consumer-and-employee-esg-
expectations.html

21. Bright Network Research, https://www.brightnetwork.co
.uk/employers/bright-network-research-report/

CHAPTER 14

Freedom to Be Human

It is said that if aliens landed on Earth and we tried to speak to them, it would be like an ant trying to speak to a human being. Our best guess is that if we met any form of advanced alien life, data and mathematics would be the most likely shared language.

For too long, employees and leaders have been like ants trying to speak to human beings. The data in this book can put leaders and employees in partnership to create workplaces where we can all thrive.

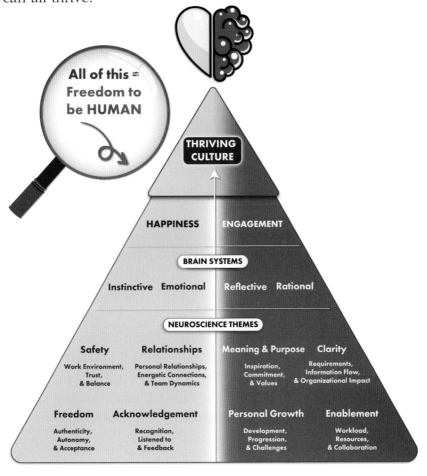

As mentioned in Chapter 1, employee happiness and engagement is a two-way street, but data can help us talk the same language.

Data Is the Plural of Anecdote

Recall that the content of this book has explored what we call the *freedom to be human* and considered 20 million data points from more than 2 million employees in more than 100 countries. We also used 223,561 employee happiness and engagement research studies, 24 in-depth expert interviews, and a deep sample of 22,000 employees.

I have always loved the saying that "data is the plural of anecdote," because it brings the storytellers and the data world together. It shows that we don't need to ignore the lived experience of individuals, while taking advantage of vast improvements in technology to help us crunch data to learn and improve the way we do things.

We Are at a Crossroads

In many ways, of course, the pandemic was a horrific time for human beings. However, it also showed how resilient and adaptable human beings can be. It showed that trusted employees (or human beings, as we like to be known) can achieve so much.

Sadly, there is now a pushback from organizations across the globe to take back control. This manifests itself in many different ways, from forcing employees back into the office to remotely tracking keystrokes to monitoring remote workers' time at their desks to using AI to track the movements of employees in a factory.

These moves are driven by a fear that employees can't be trusted. An arrogant toxic belief that employees are inherently lazy. Although most people don't state these views publicly they hide it under the blanket of culture. They say stuff like people need to be in an office to build a good culture. They prefer to tell employees what is good for them rather than listening, learning and building something new and special together.

Although the office versus work-from-home debate is an important one, it has distracted us all from the real conversation of what drives engagement and happiness. Whether you work from home, a factory, a farm, have a hybrid setup, or work completely in an office, if the eight key drivers discussed in this book are not addressed, you and your employees, teams, and company—will struggle to thrive.

Whatever the location of work our job is to provide safety, relationships, meaning and purpose, clarity, freedom, acknowledgment, personal growth, and enablement to help our people and organizations thrive.

How and where you do that should come after the plan to nurture these human needs.

This Big Brother tendency is creeping into the workplace and it is being enabled by technology. It is one of the main reasons anonymity is so integral to our work.

Like any power, technology can be used to control, but it can also be used to enhance. As Uncle Ben advised the young Peter Parker in Spider-Man, "With great power comes great responsibility."

It is clear that the working world is at a crossroads. Although guarding against dystopian states is still of significant importance to the future of humanity, there is also an equally dangerous future where organizations create highly controlled worlds where humans can be led by despotic billionaire leaders.

AI and large language models are now front and centre of this debate.

Do we want to continue on this dystopian path back to 1984, or do we want human beings someday to look back at the 2020s as the era where we started the long but important climb toward freedom?

AI can free us. It can give us our lives back by automating those tasks that mean we don't have time for our own well-being, families and friends.

AI can also be used to control us on a scale that has not been seen before. AI can be the tool that not even George Orwell predicted.

Only we as citizens of our countries and employees of our companies can decide the future. We must all educate ourselves on the true brilliant potential of AI and engage positively in the debate in how we can use it to achieve our Freedom to be human.

AI will not go away. It will shape the future of work and we are the only people who can make sure this future is a positive one. The next generation that are not even born are depending on us to do it.

Back to the Future

Shortly after my daughter Izzy was a born, I remember attending a christening of another child. As I was leaving the church, the priest blocked my way and asked my daughter if she was a pagan. Obviously she could not reply because she was a baby, and I declined to answer the priest's question. I just kept quiet and smiled. The priest went on to ask my daughter another four times if she was a pagan; eventually I walked around him in silence and left the church.

If I'm being kind, I can guess he was probably enquiring if my daughter had been baptized, surely there was a less passive-aggressive way of making that enquiry. I myself had been baptized and served as an altar boy in that very same Catholic church.

Unfortunately, my brother Kieran and I had short careers as altar boys as we were fired for one too many pranks. The straw that broke the camel's back was when it was discovered we had speeded up the Saturday night service to finish early so we could get home to watch '90s sensation Gladiators on Saturday night TV.

"Contenders, you will go on my first whistle. Gladiators, you will go on my second whistle" (read in a Scottish accent).

Who knows if I was being an overprotective dad or was holding a grudge against that church for firing me as a 12 year old boy, but the night of that baptism I went home and Googled what a pagan is.

I found this definition on the NHS website: "Pagans believe that nature is sacred and that the natural cycles of birth, growth, and death observed in the world around us carry profoundly spiritual meanings. Human beings are seen as part of nature, along with other animals, trees, stones, plants, and everything else that is of this Earth."

I wouldn't describe myself as a pagan and I'm not about to convert but I do know how disconnected the working world has become from nature and its natural cycles. We miss out on something incredibly important by not seeing ourselves as part of nature.

I believe in respecting all faiths and backgrounds, but I also believe that somewhere in the race to look upward, whether for a belief in heaven and/or the race to reach Mars, we have forgotten some important universal truths about living a happy and engaged life. As Shakespeare wrote, "It is not in the stars to hold our destiny but in ourselves."

I am a technologist and I believe in technology. However, we need technology that reconnects us with what it is to be human, now more than ever. Technology that frees up our time to spend with our loved ones and to do great work is the future. I encourage everyone reading this book to think about how they can use the data in this book to build a work culture that is more natural.

I started with small steps years ago with walking meetings, but we can do so much more and learn so much from incorporating nature into our organizations in order to grow and thrive.

People often misquote or misinterpret Charles Darwin by shortcutting the concept in their own heads that survival of the fittest means only the strong survive. We must look to nature as inspiration for how we build our future businesses and remember Darwin's full teachings: "It is not the biggest and strongest that survive, but the most adaptable to change."

The more we remove our organizations from the natural way of doing things, the more we will struggle to be part of nature and be able to adapt in an ever-changing world.

My career started in food, and the most forward-thinking farmers I know are trying to unlearn harmful industrial approaches to farming and instead work with nature as opposed to against it. They are doing this to simultaneously feed the world and also to protect the planet. These two seemingly opposing views are being realigned to build a brighter future for all of us.

This approach to regenerative farming can also be used to shape our thinking in all sectors. Some of the most innovative corporate organizations are applying regenerative thinking to build new ways of working.

It is time to stop seeing employees like industrial batteries that you simply exhaust and chuck away, and start treating them as part of an ecosystem that needs nurturing and regenerating.

Data and technology can help us relearn and better understand what is needed to thrive as human beings.

The Future and Technology

Technology has given us so much to advance ourselves as human beings: penicillin, AI, Google Maps, space travel, *The Emoji Movie*.... Nowadays, the working world is so connected that we can have a video call with another human being instantaneously almost anywhere in the world at any time.

Evolution occurs over thousands of years through natural selection, and not over decades because of technology. This fundamental truth means there is not much difference between us and our forebears from before the industrial revolution. We are currently going through the fourth industrial revolution, called the digital revolution, but we are still the same human beings that lived a few thousand years ago.

If we disconnect ourselves from nature a fourth time, we once again lose part of what makes us human. We lose what it is to be human. We don't expect plants to grow without the right components such as light and healthy soil, and we should not expect our employees to grow without creating the right environment to thrive.

The meaning of life?

I no longer ask myself, "What is the meaning of life?" I firmly believe that the meaning of life is simply finding meaning in life.

There are many ways that organizations can help their employees find meaning in their work and their lives. The journey starts by listening to your employees and by working hard to align your employees' aims with the vision of the organization.

If we can reconnect with the natural world, we will not only thrive and help protect this amazing planet, but can ultimately be adaptable to change, and lead us into a future where two plus two can equal four.

"Freedom is the freedom to say that two plus two make four. If that is granted all else follows."

Today, this is about giving employees a voice to help positively shape the future of their organizations. This needs to be on everything from AI to Gender to Racial Equity.

We call this *the freedom to be human.*

The future

Organizations can change the world. You can change the world. This book has outlined the conditions needed for employees and therefore human beings to thrive. The emotions your employees feel today are a guide to the performance of your organization tomorrow. If nurtured they can be harnessed to drive success.

Our collective emotions can be more powerful than any technology we can ever invent. Let's stop ignoring them and use them to create a more humane future.

I will let you decide what you do with this information....

About the Author

I am a dad, founder, CEO, board advisor, author, and TEDx speaker.

My career started with working on a farm. My first venture outside of that was founding a digital marketing agency called 4Ps Marketing when I was 25 years old. Chris Hyland and I started 4Ps in an attic on Wimpole Street in London and went on to service over 100 iconic brands, including Selfridges, Marks & Spencer, Nissan, and L'Oréal, before exiting the business via a trade sale.

I still hold a keen interest in food: where we source it, how we grow it, and ultimately how we can feed ourselves in a regenerative way.

My desire to better understand culture and what connects us became part of the founding story of The Happiness Index, alongside Chris and Tony Latter. My day-to-day role as co-CEO of The Happiness Index is focused on helping us move toward our vision, which we describe as "Freedom to Be Human." I am also a global advisor to organizations and keynote speaker at some of the world's most important conferences.

I believe the well-being of humans and the planet are inextricably linked. I hope the work in this book helps improve the daily lives of ordinary people just like you and me.

Index